Treasury of Love Proverbs
from Many Lands

Treasury of Love Proverbs from Many Lands

The Editors at Hippocrene Books
Illustrations by Rosemary Fox

HIPPOCRENE
New York

For information, address:
HIPPOCRENE BOOKS, INC.
171 Madison Avenue
New York, NY 10016

Library of Congress Cataloging-in-Publication Data

Treasury of love proverbs from many lands / the editors of Hippocrene
    Books ; illustrations by Rosemary Fox.
        p.   cm.
    Includes bibliographical references and index.
    ISBN 0-7818-0563-5
    1. Love--Quotations, maxims, etc. 2. Proverbs. I. Hippocrene
    Books (Firm)
    PN6525.L68T74   1997
    302.3--dc21   97-32213
                                                               CIP

Printed in the United States of America.

CONTENTS

Love's strength is truth.
(Russia)

Treasury of Love Proverbs from Many Lands

LOVE DEFINED

1. *At birth love is blind like a kitten, but as it grows older it receives a hundred eyes. (Finland)*

2. *Love is a bad neighbor, but to have none is worse. (Spain)*

3. *Love is a blind guide and those who follow him often lose their way. (Italy)*

4. *Love is a circle and an endless sphere. (Russia)*

5. *Love is a disease, but it does not want to be healed. (Czech Republic)*

6. *Love is a flower garden and marriage is a field of nettles. (Finland)*

7. *Love is a friendship set afire. (United States)*

8. *Love is a little sighing and a little lying. (United States)*

9. *Love is a metal pot: off the fire it cools at once. (Swahili)*

10. *Love is a ring and a ring has no beginning and no end. (Russia)*

11. *Love is a sweet dream and marriage is the alarm clock. (Hebrew)*

12. *Love is blind and cannot see the pretty follies which lovers themselves commit. (Italy)*

13. *Love is blind and thinks others don't see either. (Denmark)*

14. *Love is blind but can see far away. (Italy)*

15. *Love is blind but marriage restores one's vision. (Italy)*

16. *Love is blind, that's why you have to touch. (Brazil)*

17. *Love is blind—but not the neighbors. (Mexico)*

18. *Love is blinding. That is why lovers like to touch. (Germany)*

19. *Love is born by curiosity, endures by habit. (Italy)*

20. *Love is born of love. (Poland)*

21. *Love is cunning, it wears golden fetters. (Hungary)*

22. *Love is full of honey and gall. (Slovenia)*

23. *Love is heavy, but lack of love is heavier. (Russia)*

24. *Love is impatient. (Ukraine)*

25. *Love is like a baby: it needs to be treated tenderly. (Congo)*

26. *Love is like a color which fades away. (Shona)*

27. *Love is like a good horse, it carries the man. (Ukraine)*

28. *Love is like a mousetrap: you go in when you want, but you don't get out when you like. (Spain)*

29. *Love is like butter, it's good with bread. (Yiddish)*

30. *Love is like fog, there is no mountain on which it does not rest. (Hawaiian)*

31. *Love is like glass that breaks if handled clumsily. (Russia)*

32. *Love is like rice: if you plant it elsewhere it will also grow. (Madagascar)*

33. *Love is like the moon: if it doesn't get bigger, it gets smaller. (Portugual)*

34. *Love is like war: you begin when you like and leave off when you can. (Spain)*

35. *Love is never without troubles. (Italy)*

36. *Love is not based on wealth. (Twi)*

37. *Love is not found in the market. (Russia)*

38. *Love is nourished by mutual sacrifice. (Italy)*

39. *Love is often bitter, but it reassures the heart. (Italy)*

40. *Love is often the fruit of marriage. (France)*

41. *Love is one-eyed; hate is blind. (Denmark)*

42. *Love is only a portion of a man's life, but it is the whole of a woman's life. (Italy)*

43. *Love is only love when it affects both sides. (Swahili)*

44. *Love is severe and devotion tough, it kills you on your feet and the eyes remain open. (Finland)*

45. *Love is sometimes difficult, but death even more so. (Albania)*

46. *Love is sweet, but it's nice to have bread with it. (Yiddish)*

47. *Love is sweet, love is poison. (Swahili)*

48. *Love is the beginning of sorrow. (Germany)*

Love is the greatest of all virtues. (Twi)

49. *Love is the greatest of all virtues. (Twi)*

50. *Love is the longing to achieve another's happiness by achieving our own. (France)*

51. *Love is the sister of madness. (Malta)*

52. *Love is works not words. (Spain)*

53. *Love without jealousy is like a Pole without a mustache. (Poland)*

54. *Love without money is a gate to misery. (Poland)*

55. *Love without reciprocity is a question without an answer. (Germany)*

56. *Love without strife is love that is smoldering. (Italy)*

57. *What love is, is peace. (Myanmar)*

KINDS OF LOVE

58. *A girl's love, luck in cards, the squire's favor, and the rose's bloom don't last. (Poland)*

59. *A nun's love is a raging inferno. (Spain)*

60. *A secret love is always a true love. (Slovakia)*

61. *A shameful love is usually deaf. (Latin)*

62. *A small love forgives much, a great love forgives little, and a perfect love forgives all. (United States)*

63. *Carnal love is stronger than sacramental love. (Malta)*

64. *Children's love is like water in a basket. (Argentina)*

65. *Extreme love brings extreme hatred. (Oromo)*

66. *Forced love and painted cheeks don't last. (Germany)*

67. *Forced love does not last. (Holland)*

68. *Great love form little things may grow. (Canada)*

69. *Hot love is soon cold. (Poland)*

70. *Love blinds itself to all shortcomings. (Lebanon)*

71. New loves come and go, an old love remains. *(Italy)*
72. Old love does not rust. *(Germany)*
73. Old love is easily kindled. *(Canada)*
74. Old loves are never forgotten. *(Italy)*
75. Perfect love casts out all fears. *(Italy)*
76. Perfect love sometimes does not come until the first grandchild. *(Wales)*
77. Physical or dishonest love is obscene and damaging. *(Poland)*
78. Real love is when you don't have to tell each other. *(France)*
79. True love can never become old. *(Italy)*

LOVE AND...

80. Love and a cough cannot be hidden. *(Latin)*
81. Love and anger are not fair judges. *(Hungary)*
82. Love and death know no limits. *(Russia)*
83. Love and eggs are best when they are fresh. *(Russia)*
84. Love and eggs should be fresh to be enjoyed. *(United States)*
85. Love and fear exclude each other. *(Latin)*
86. Love and fear never go together. *(Latvia)*
87. Love and hate are the two closest emotions. *(United States)*
88. Love and hunger don't dwell together. *(Yiddish)*
89. Love and lordship like no fellowship. *(Poland)*
90. Love and mastery are not companions. *(Italy)*
91. Love and scandal are the best sweeteners of tea. *(United States)*
92. Love and smoke cannot be hidden. *(Russia)*
93. Love and the nobility don't tolerate sharing. *(Hungary)*
94. Love and the weather can never be depended upon. *(United States)*
95. Love, smoke, and coughing cannot be hidden. *(Hungary)*

Love and eggs should be fresh to be enjoyed. (United States)

96. *Love, wine, and gambling empty the purse.* (Hungary)
97. *To tell the truth, love and reason are seldom seen in the same company.* (Italy)

LOVE'S ACTIONS

98. *Beauty does not grow love, love grows beauty.* (Poland)
99. *Give love free reign and it will lead you into slavery.* (Ukraine)
100. *Hate calls for disputes, love conquers all offenses.* (Czech Republic)
101. *It's love that makes the seashell stick to the rock.* (Twi)
102. *Love begins with song and dance and ends in a sea of tears.* (Italy)
103. *Love begins with the eyes.* (Russia)
104. *Love blinds your eyes, marriage opens them wide.* (Finland)
105. *Love brings forth many heroes, but even more idiots.* (Sweden)
106. *Love brings the distant near.* (France)
107. *Love can do a lot, money still more.* (Spain)
108. *Love can make any place agreeable.* (United States)
109. *Love can tear you from a rosary to a dance.* (Poland)
110. *Love conceals all of one's faults.* (Italy)
111. *Love consumes understanding.* (Luganda)
112. *Love creates love in response.* (Germany)
113. *Love cures coquetry.* (United States)
114. *Love delights in praise.* (England)
115. *Love deprives the wise of half their wit, fools of everything.* (Finland)
116. *Love does much; money does everything.* (Italy)
117. *Love does not look but sees everything.* (Russia)
118. *Love does not measure distance.* (Finland)
119. *Love does not recognize the law.* (Portugual)

Love can tear you from a rosary to a dance. (Poland)

120. *Love endures many delays. (France)*

121. *Love engenders love. (France)*

122. *Love enters man through his eyes, woman through her ears. (United States)*

123. *Love feeds without bread. (Poland)*

124. *Love fills the world and multiplies heaven. (Germany)*

125. *Love goes where it's sent. (Canada)*

126. *Love has a long nose. (Poland)*

127. *Love intoxicates a man; marriage sobers him. (United States)*

128. *Love kills with golden arrows. (Spain)*

129. *Love knows no dangers. (Poland)*

130. *Love knows no difference between high and low. (Japan)*

131. *Love knows no hidden paths. (Germany)*

132. *Love laughs at locksmiths. (England)*

133. *Love lives in cottages as well as in courts. (England)*

134. *Love lives on hope and dies with it. (Poland)*

135. *Love makes a man blind and deaf. (Saudi Arabia)*

136. *Love makes cottages manors; straw, silken ribbons. (Estonia)*

137. *Love makes labor light. (Holland)*

138. *Love makes time pass; time makes love pass. (France)*

139. *Love needs quarrel. (Germany)*

140. *Love no longer lives when hope is dead. (Italy)*

141. *Love perceives nothing as labor. (Italy)*

142. *Love produces heroes, but also idiots. (Denmark)*

143. *Love pulls as hard as five teams of oxen. (Finland)*

144. *Love redeems many sins. (Russia)*

145. *Love rules his kingdom without a sword. (Italy)*

146. *Love rules without any laws. (Italy)*

147. *Love scorns duty. (Poland)*

Love lives in cottages as well as in courts. (England)

148. *Love sweetens everything. (Poland)*

149. *Love teaches even donkeys to dance. (France)*

150. *Love understands all languages. (Romania)*

151. *Love will creep where it cannot go. (England)*

152. *Love will creep where it may not go. (Germany)*

153. *Love without gifts does not become evident at all. (Swahili)*

154. *Tenderness causes love and love causes doltishness. (China)*

155. *The greatness of love obliterates conventions. (Sudan)*

ATTRACTION AND FLIRTATION

156. *A handsome finger gets a ring put around it. (Swahili)*

157. *A lovely girl attracts attention by her good looks, an ugly girl by the help of a mirror. (Malta)*

158. *A pampered girl may not get a husband of her choice. (Kashmiri)*

159. *A pole is not a spear, seduction is not the same as wedlock. (Swahili)*

160. *A pretty face needs no adornment. (Swahili)*

161. *Beauty without chastity is a flower without smell. (Tamil)*

162. *Dancing is the way to make you famous and to get the girl you desire. (Turkana)*

163. *Even horses kick when in love. (Finland)*

164. *Getting engaged is not hard, paying the money is. (Hausa)*

165. *Happy is the wooing that is not long in doing. (England)*

166. *He that would the daughter win, must with the mother first begin. (England)*

167. *He who is not melted by anything else may be melted by love. (Tamil)*

168. *Love at a distance stays warm the longest. (Germany)*

169. *Love if you want to be loved. (Latin)*

Dancing is the way to make you famous and to get the girl you desire. (Turkana)

170. Neither do I want honey nor the sting of the bee. *(Kashmiri)*

171. No one hates beauty, but beauty hates someone. *(Oromo)*

172. One does not notice the faults of the person one loves. *(Malta)*

173. The language of love is in the eyes. *(Italy)*

174. There are no such things as nice prisons and ugly loves. *(France)*

175. Though your friendship reach her bosom, don't put your hand on her bosom. *(Tamil)*

176. With eyes you will win love. *(Lithuania)*

BEWARE OF LOVE

177. A love match without means of support recoils on the makers. *(Hausa)*

178. Before you love, learn to run through snow without leaving footprints. *(Turkey)*

179. Don't be so much in love that you can't tell when it's raining. *(Madagascar)*

180. Don't believe in pillow talk. *(Luyia)*

181. For a little love you pay all your life. *(Yiddish)*

182. Hugging does not cure desire. *(Finland)*

183. In the face of love and death, courage is useless. *(Spain)*

184. Infatuation is faster than a horse with a tail shorter than a sheep's. *(Tibet)*

185. Love and let everyone know; hate and be silent. *(Egypt)*

186. Love but do not fall in love. *(Russia)*

187. Love does not choose the blade of grass on which it falls. *(Zulu)*

188. Love has neither eyes nor understanding. *(Swahili)*

189. Love has no light, pity has no rays. *(Malta)*

190. Love is worse than a sickness when it gives no peace. *(Ukraine)*

191. Loving with the eyes only has blinded a lot of fools. *(France)*

192. *One cannot love and be wise. (Poland)*

193. *The crowning moment of our life, happiness without peace, this is love. (Italy)*

194. *The gain of love is little, is little. (Swahili)*

195. *The lover of a student does not always become the wife of a graduate. (Mexico)*

196. *There are three things that can never be hidden—love, a mountain, and one riding on a camel. (Saudi Arabia)*

197. *They love too much that die for love. (England)*

198. *Who writes love letters grows thin; who carries them, fat. (Holland)*

199. *You know sweetness can kill, so why have you given me poison? (Swahili)*

UNREQUITED LOVE

200. *A bachelor should not woo a woman for another man. (Dagari)*

201. *But alas, if one lacks the resources one cannot even bite the palm of one's own hand. (Tibet)*

202. *He came to ask for her hand and returned with a pumpkin. (Ukraine)*

203. *He that gives the laws of love is usually a bachelor. (United States)*

204. *He who finds not love finds nothing. (Spain)*

205. *He who forces love where none is found remains a fool the whole year round. (United States)*

206. *He who loves me, I also love him; he who rejects me diminishes my grief. (Swahili)*

207. *It is as difficult to win love as it is to pack salt in pine needles. (Myanmar)*

208. *It is better to love someone you cannot have than have someone you cannot love. (United States)*

209. *Love can neither be bought nor sold. (Ukraine)*

210. Love can't be begged for, nor threatened for. *(Czech Republic)*
211. Loving one who loves another is a bellyful of trouble. *(Hausa)*
212. The extent of my love for you is buried in stone. *(Luganda)*
213. There is no love so true as one which dies untold. *(Italy)*
214. To give love to one who loves you not is like rain falling on the desert. *(Swahili)*
215. To love someone who does not love you is like shaking a tree to make the dew drops fall. *(Congo)*
216. Vows of love and smoke from the fireplace, the wind blows them both away. *(Spain)*
217. When we cannot get what we love, we must love what is within our reach. *(France)*
218. White ants do not really love the dry stalk of corn: those we think love us, love us only a little. *(Yoruba)*
219. You cannot threaten someone to love you. *(Poland)*

END OR ABSENCE OF LOVE

220. A life without love is like a year without summer. *(Sweden)*
221. A lone hand does not applaud. *(Wolof)*
222. A love defined is a love that is finished. *(France)*
223. A spinster is like an old letter that was written, and was never sent. *(Hungary)*
224. Faults are thick where love is thin. *(Denmark)*
225. Great love is followed by great hate. *(Georgia)*
226. He who deserts his household will be deserted by them. *(Hausa)*
227. Love never dies of starvation, but often of indigestion. *(France)*
228. No fate is worse than a life without love. *(Mexico)*

To love someone who does not love you is like shaking a tree to make the dew drops fall. (Congo)

229. Not to have been loved is a misfortune, but not to have loved is a tragedy. (Italy)

230. Poverty does not let you know the one who might love you. (Luganda)

231. Pretense of love is worse than hatred. (Latin)

232. Short love, long sighs. (Romania)

233. The end of passion is the beginning of repentance. (France)

234. With hungry people love cannot last long. (Poland)

235. Without wine and food even love grows pale. (Italy)

236. You cannot bring back love or life. (Swahili)

237. You will not be loved if you think yourself alone. (Italy)

FIRST LOVE & NEW LOVE

238. A character full of love is like a river without a wave. (Tamil)

239. A silent passion increases more ardently. (Italy)

240. Affection is like glue or varnish. (China)

241. Do not be put off by a partner's poor dancing. (Luyia)

242. Eating comes before being in love. (Japan)

243. First love letters are written with the eye. (France)

244. It doesn't cost anything to promise and to love. (Yiddish)

245. Let your love be like a torrent: Heavy at first but swiftly abating. Let your love be like drizzle: it comes softly, but still swells the river. (Madagascar)

246. Love at first sight is often extinguished by the second. (Germany)

247. Love at first sight is the most common eye disease. (Germany)

248. Love, pain, and money cannot be kept secret; they soon betray themselves. (Spain)

249. "No more trouble," you say when the one you love arrives. (Luganda)

250. Nobody's sweetheart is ugly. (Holland)

Do not be put off by a partner's poor dancing. (Luyia)

251. One always returns to one's first love. (France)
252. Rings make a sound if there are two. (Zulu)
253. Sorrow is weightless; you carry your first love to your grave. (Ukraine)
254. That which is loved is always beautiful. (Norway)
255. The look of love slices through all faults. (Wolof)
256. The love of one's youth and Christmas cheese will always be remembered. (Finland)
257. The magic of the first love is the ignorance that it can never end. (Italy)
258. The new one is the loved one. (Nembe)
259. The one you love is always wished success. (Haya)
260. The torch of love is lit in the kitchen. (France)
261. The weather is always fair when people are in love. (Italy)
262. Those in love need only the smallest of places. (Luganda)
263. Those whom we love first, we seldom wed. (United States)
264. You cannot hide light nor love. (Ukraine)

KISS

265. A kiss of the mouth often touches not the heart. (England)
266. A kiss tells more than a whole book. (Ukraine)
267. A kiss without a beard is like an egg without salt. (Holland)
268. A kiss without a hug is like a flower without a fragrance. (Malta)
269. A lisping lass is good to kiss. (England)
270. For luve o' the nurse mony ane kisses the bairn. (Scotland)
271. In love there is always one who kisses and one who offers the cheek. (France)
272. It's a pitiful kiss, if you have to pay for it. (Hungary)

In love there is always one who kisses and one who offers the cheek. (France)

273. *Kisses are like almonds. (Malta)*

274. *Kisses are not for nothing. (Hungary)*

275. *Let us eat borshch; as for the meat we will give each other a kiss. (Ukraine)*

276. *Many are betrayed with a kiss. (Russia)*

277. *The sound of a kiss is not as strong as that of a canon but its echo may endure much longer. (Italy)*

PAIN OF LOVE

278. *A quarrel is the renewing of love. (Italy)*

279. *Fear and love never go together. (Italy)*

280. *For the disease of love there is no cure. (Swahili)*

281. *He who loves you brings you joy, but in the end he will make you cry. (Malta)*

282. *In love all is sadness; but sadness and all, it's still the best thing in life. (Spain)*

283. *In war, hunting, and love a little pleasure gives a lot of pain. (Spain)*

284. *It is best to love wisely, no doubt, but to love foolishly is better than not to love at all. (Italy)*

285. *It's better to eat dry bread in love than a feast in sorrow. (Spain)*

286. *Love lasts as long as does the reproach. (Saudi Arabia)*

287. *Love me less, but love me for a long time. (Yiddish)*

288. *Love, your pains are worth more than all other pleasures combined. (France)*

289. *Mistakes made for love are worthy of forgiveness. (Spain)*

290. *"No more joy," you say when the one you love goes to war. (Luganda)*

291. *That which does not go away in tears, goes away in sighs. (Cuba)*

292. *The greater the love the greater the obstacle. (Poland)*

The sound of a kiss is not as strong as that of a canon but its echo may endure much longer. (Italy)

293. *The love that you die from is too big. (France)*

294. *The more violent the love, the more violent the anger. (Myanmar)*

295. *The one who truly loves you will cause you pain. (Spain)*

296. *They love too much that die for love. (Canada)*

297. *To love is to deny oneself. (Latin)*

298. *True love never runs smooth. (Canada)*

299. *Try to reason about love and you will lose your reason. (France)*

300. *Who loves well is ready to forgive. (Ukraine)*

JEALOUSY

301. *A jealous lover becomes an indifferent spouse. (Mexico)*

302. *A jealous woman keeps the whole house on fire. (Ukraine)*

303. *Disquiet is the constant companion of jealousy. (Philippines)*

304. *Estrangement springs from jealousy. (China)*

305. *If jealousy caused hunger, then all men would be hungry. (Twi)*

306. *Jealousy can be as cruel as death. (Italy)*

307. *Jealousy does not grow old. (Wales)*

308. *Jealousy is a pain that eagerly seeks what causes pain. (Germany)*

309. *Jealousy is the life of love. (Japan)*

310. *Love cannot dwell with suspicion. (United States)*

311. *Love has sharp vision, hate's is sharper, but jealousy's is sharpest because it combines love and hate. (Saudi Arabia)*

312. *Love is never without jealousy. (Poland)*

313. *Love is too rare to lose to jealousy. (Mexico)*

314. *On the cliff of jealousy the tender shoots of merit will not grow. (Tibet)*

315. *The result of love is jealousy and broken faith. (Italy)*

316. *There is no cure for jealousy. (China)*

HEART

317. *A broken hand works, but not a broken heart. (Iran)*

318. *A broken heart is like broken china: we can mend it, but we can never erase the scars. (United States)*

319. *A faint heart never won a fair lady. (Poland)*

320. *A heart without love is a violin without strings. (United States)*

321. *A kind heart is better than a crafty head. (Isle of Man)*

322. *A letter from the heart can be read on the face. (Swahili)*

323. *A loving heart can also reject. (Swahili)*

324. *A loving heart is better and stronger than wisdom. (United States)*

325. *A loving heart is not to be argued with. (Swahili)*

326. *A man's heart at thirty is either steeled or broken. (United States)*

327. *A man's heart changes as often as does the autumn sky. (Japan)*

328. *A pain in the bone is better than a pain in the heart. (Cuba)*

329. *Affection that is genuine never turns a heart into a stone. (Tibet)*

330. *Allah gives to us according to the measure of our hearts. (Iran)*

331. *As a man's heart is, so does he speak. (Sanskrit)*

332. *Cultivate a heart of love that knows no anger. (Cambodia)*

333. *Every heart has its own ache. (Canada)*

334. *Every man has three ears: one on the left side of his head, one on the right, and one in his heart. (Armenia)*

335. *Faint heart ne'er wan fair lady. (Scotland)*

336. *Far from the eye, far from the heart. (Malta)*

337. *For news of the heart ask the face. (Guinea)*

338. *He who loves with his heart finds the words to say it. (Ukraine)*

339. *He whose heart is aroused by love will never die. (Iran)*

340. *Hearts don't break, they bend and wither. (United States)*

341. *If the eyes do not see, the heart does not cry. (Ukraine)*

342. *If you are bitter in the heart, sugar in the mouth will not help you. (Yiddish)*

343. *If you cannot build a town, build a heart. (Kurdistan)*

344. *In sickness of the heart, it is the medicine of love that can affect a cure. (China)*

345. *It is better to be embarrassed than heartbroken. (Yiddish)*

346. *It is not I, it is my heart. (Swahili)*

347. *Let the heart that will not glow, slumber. (Wales)*

348. *Let your heart rule your head in matters of affection. (United States)*

349. *Like a face reflecting itself in water, so does man reflect his heart. (Czech Republic)*

350. *Love governs the heart, resentments drive the mind. (Poland)*

351. *Love is the one who enters someone's heart, even if it is taboo. (Tsonga)*

352. *Love makes all hard hearts gentle. (Poland)*

353. *Love that blushes is a flower; love that pales, a tragedy of the heart. (Belgium)*

354. *Many a heart is caught on the rebound. (United States)*

355. *Nobody dies of a broken heart. (United States)*

356. *One cannot make laws to rule the heart. The power of love cannot be compelled. (Italy)*

357. *Only the heart can find the way to another heart. (Iran)*

358. *Out of the abundance of the heart the mouth speaks. (Holland)*

359. *Straw in your shoe and love in your heart will always show. (Germany)*

360. *Stronger even than stone is a man's heart. (Bulgaria)*

361. *The eye runs to what is dear to the heart. (Ukraine)*

362. *The hand to the nail and the heart to the beloved. (Hindi)*

363. *The heart desires that which is out of reach. (Luyia)*

364. *The heart does not grieve over what the eyes have not seen. (Slovakia)*

365. *The heart does not lie. (Holland)*

366. *The heart has arguments with which the understanding is acquainted. (United States)*

367. *The heart has eyes that the brain knows nothing of. (United States)*

368. *The heart has no wrinkles. (United States)*

369. *The heart is but the beach beside the sea that is the world. (China)*

370. *The heart is its own witness. (Tamil)*

371. *The heart is mad: it falls in love with one who is another's. (Yaka)*

372. *The heart is small and embraces the whole wide world. (Yiddish)*

373. *The heart knows its own bitterness. (United States)*

374. *The heart of a human being is as deep as a well. (Swahili)*

375. *The heart of a man may be compared to a sausage: no one can tell exactly what's inside. (Yiddish)*

376. *The heart that loves is always young. (Greece)*

377. *The heart's wishes are like a horse galloping on the open sky. (Tibet)*

378. *The human heart is neither of stone nor wood. (Japan)*

379. *The mouth is the interpreter of the heart. (Estonia)*

380. *The power of love is determined by the strength the heart has given to it. (Italy)*

381. *The road to a heart is only known by another heart. (Ukraine)*

382. *The tongue is the interpreter of the heart. (Egypt)*

383. *The way to a man's heart is through his ego. (United States)*

384. *Three things refresh the heart: water, flowers, and a beautiful face. (Swahili)*

385. *Trouble cuts up the heart. (Yiddish)*

386. *Two hearts never beat the same. (United States)*

387. *When the heart is at ease the body is healthy. (China)*

388. *With familiarity even a tiger engenders no fear in a girl's heart. (Tibet)*

389. *Words from the heart reach the heart, words form the mouth reach the ear. (Saudi Arabia)*

390. *You can peek into houses but not hearts. (Maori)*

LOVERS

391. *A lover has no grudge. (Swahili)*

392. *A lover who loves you not is like the calf of your leg which turns its back on whatever side your stomach turns to. (Luganda)*

393. *All the world loves a lover. (Russia)*

394. *Being loved is the best way of being useful. (France)*

395. *Better an ugly love from your village, than a beauty from an unknown one. (Romania)*

396. *Carry on with your lover as you tend your flock. (Masai)*

397. *Don't just take love, experience it. (Iran)*

398. *For those in love, Baghdad is near Istanbul. (Turkey)*

399. *He who does not love does not strive. (Latin)*

400. *He who loves thinks the others are blind; the others think he is crazy. (Saudi Arabia)*

401. *He who loves you is worth loving. (Malta)*

402. *He who treads the path of love walks a thousand meters as if it were only one. (Japan)*

403. *He who waits for his lover hears the footsteps of the spirits. (Igbo)*

404. *If you make love in the shade you get cold. (Japan)*

405. *In the war of love, the one who flees wins. (Italy)*

406. *Just because my girlfriend is beautiful, it doesn't mean I'll climb a pear tree protected with charms. (Igbo)*

407. *Just because your lover has come, honey won't turn into mead. (Oromo)*

408. *Lovers always find a place to meet. (Ukraine)*

409. *Lovers do not hide their nakedness. (the Congo)*

410. *Lovers swear that everyone else is blind. (Spain)*

411. *Lucky is he who knew reciprocal love or none at all. (Poland)*

412. *Once a lover, always a lover. (United States)*

413. One cannot hide love from a lover's eyes. (Italy)

414. One does not strip a maiden of her clothes and sit gazing into her eyes. (Yoruba)

415. One lover, that is love; two lovers, that is passion; three lovers, that is commerce. (France)

416. One who tries to unite prudence and love knows nothing about love. (Italy)

417. One who truly loves finds it difficult to forget. (Spain)

418. One who wants to be a lover must be brave. (Italy)

419. Rose water is not for the backs of old folk, but for the breasts of young lovers. (Iran)

420. Someone in love is drunk. (Swahili)

421. Tell me whom you love, and I'll tell you who you are. (United States)

422. The anger of lovers lasts a short time. (Italy)

423. The lover who gives you her body but not her heart is generous with thornless roses. (Iran)

424. The lover who hurts is the only one who can heal. (Germany)

425. The one you love is never blemished by disease. (Yoruba)

426. The sight of lovers feeds those in love. (United States)

427. The tears of one who loves will come even from a bad eye. (Swahili)

428. The way is never long to one's beloved. (Poland)

429. Those who love you will make you weep; those who hate you will make you laugh. (Russia)

430. To love someone truly you have to love them as if your beloved were to die tomorrow. (Saudi Arabia)

431. Tomorrow shall be love for the loveless and for the lover tomorrow shall be love. (Latin)

432. True lovers are always shy when people are by. (United States)

433. Two lovers in the rain have no need of an umbrella. (Japan)

434. What a woman eats, a man eats too; what a man eats, so will a woman. (Yaka)

435. *What you handle gently is never spoiled; what you handle roughly causes grief. (Yoruba)*

436. *You'd even build your house on a hard rock for someone who loves you. (Luganda)*

437. *Your mistress's visit brings you good luck. (Malta)*

WOMAN

438. *A cock chases the rain with its tail, a woman shows her love towards her husband in small talk. (Yaka)*

439. *A helpless woman will get a foolish husband. (Telugu)*

440. *A hero cannot get out of the influence of women. (China)*

441. *A king will not divorce a woman only for a poverty-stricken man to marry her. (Yoruba)*

442. *A woman can't drive her husband, but she can lead him. (Germany)*

443. *A woman cannot be proud of her husband unless he gives her children. (Kaonde)*

444. *A woman married without her consent runs away without consent. (Oromo)*

445. *A woman who admits she is in the wrong won't want for a husband. (Hausa)*

446. *A woman who has not lived with two husbands will never know which is the better. (Yoruba)*

447. *A woman who moves from husband to husband has no manners. (Luyia)*

448. *A woman without jewelry is a plain nun. (Tibet)*

449. *A woman's fate is determined by the love she accepts. (Italy)*

450. *An honorable woman doesn't flirt. (Swahili)*

451. *An old woman without her mate is like borshch without bread. (Ukraine)*

A woman's fate is determined by the love she accepts. (Italy)

452. *An old woman, a chaste wife. (Sanskrit)*

453. *Any old woman, if she marries, is a bride. (Hungary)*

454. *At night all women are alike. (Malta)*

455. *Declarations of a woman's love should be written in water and her promises scribbled in the sand. (Italy)*

456. *Divorced women know no constant companion. (Tibet)*

457. *Even the goddess of pestilence passes over the woman unloved by her husband. (Telugu)*

458. *Eyes never see a beautiful woman without greeting her. (Yoruba)*

459. *For women, there is no good in life except love. (Italy)*

460. *Gold and women rule the world. (Ukraine)*

461. *He who loves a woman is a nephew of the sun. (Kurdistan)*

462. *I have no desire of husband, said the nine-times married woman. (Oromo)*

463. *If a man could survive without a woman, God would not have created Eve. (Ukraine)*

464. *In her first passion woman loves her lover, in all others she is in love with love. (Italy)*

465. *In the absence of men all women are chaste. (Sanskrit)*

466. *Man is fire, woman dry straw, then the devil comes along and blows. (Spain)*

467. *One woman is like a hundred-branched maple tree to you, another is like a bitch at the door. (Kashmiri)*

468. *Satisfy a dog with a bone; a woman with a lie. (Basque)*

469. *Smart women love foolish men. (German)*

470. *Take an excellent woman even from a bad caste. (Sanskrit)*

471. *The beauty of a woman is attributed to her husband. (Twi)*

472. *The good looks of a woman are her dowry. (Malta)*

473. *The only merit of a man is his good sense, but the greatest merit of a woman is her beauty. (Italy)*

474. *To love a woman who scorns you is to lick honey from a thorn. (Wales)*

Man is fire, woman dry straw, then the devil comes along and blows. (Spain)

❁❁❁❁❁❁❁❁❁❁❁❁❁❁❁❁❁❁❁❁❁❁❁❁❁❁<

475. *True paradise is not in the heavens but upon the mouth of a woman in love. (Italy)*

476. *Whom on earth will a handsome woman not subdue? (Sanskrit)*

477. *Woman without man is like fire without wood. (Spain)*

478. *Women say a lover comes while grain is mashing. (Oromo)*

479. *Your hypocrisy is like that of a woman who carries her husband and her co-wife on her back. (Fulfulde)*

MAN

480. *A man afraid to join the army and a lazy woman are made for each other. (Luganda)*

481. *A man has eyes to look; a woman has eyes to be looked at. (Ukraine)*

482. *A man if loved, should love. (Swahili)*

483. *A man in love mistakes a harelip for a dimple. (Japan)*

484. *A man is attractive when he is not your husband. (Shona)*

485. *A man no longer married is more dangerous than one not yet married. (Hausa)*

486. *A man who makes a fool of himself on account of a woman is done for. (Malta)*

487. *A man with two wives will die of hunger or a curse. (Oromo)*

488. *A man without a woman is a tree without leaves and branches. (Italy)*

489. *A man's best fortune or his worst is his wife. (Kannada)*

490. *A poor man's love is never seen. (Swahili)*

491. *An old man in love is like a flower in winter. (Portugal)*

492. *Better to be an old man's sweetheart than a young man's slave. (England)*

493. *Even if man would be fully satisfied with everything else, he will always crave more love. (Czech Republic)*

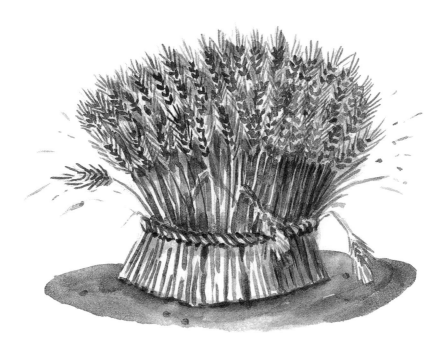

Women say a lover comes while grain is mashing. (Oromo)

494. *For every ugly man there are a pair of foolish eyes. (Malta)*

495. *It is a lonesome washing without a man's shirt in it. (Ireland)*

496. *It is better to throw oneself into a well than to marry an old man. (Tamil)*

497. *It's an inexperienced man who marries a barren woman. (Tibet)*

498. *Men may look alike but their hearts differ. (Tibet)*

499. *Money alone does not make a man rich. (Turkana)*

500. *The handsome man is king, if there is no rich man near. (Hausa)*

501. *The poor man marries a pregnant woman. (Oromo)*

502. *Time reveals a man's heart. (China)*

503. *Victory makes a man popular, and to fall in love means to be conquered. (Swahili)*

BRIDE & BRIDEGROOM

504. *A bride's eyes pretend not to see. (Luyia)*

505. *A fair bride needs little finery. (Norway)*

506. *All brides are beautiful. All dead are pious. (Yiddish)*

507. *An impatient bridegroom ties the head ornaments to his knees. (Marathi)*

508. *He that has luck leads the bride to church. (Holland)*

509. *He for whom a bride is being sought does not stretch his neck. (Yoruba)*

510. *The bride's culture can be judged by her conduct at the marriage ceremony. (Konkani)*

511. *The bridegroom strong and healthy and the bride tender and sweet, make a good match. (Konkani)*

512. *The daughter-in-law enters the house, and the mother-in-law enters the Ganges. (Telugu)*

513. *Whatever a new bride touches is fragrant. (Malta)*

514. *Woe to the high-spirited bride whose mother-in-law is still alive. (the Congo)*

WIFE

515. *A blind man's wife is God's keeping. (Kashmiri)*

516. *A good wife is a blessing, and a bad one is a curse. (Kashmiri)*

517. *A good wife is a goodly prize. (Poland)*

518. *A good wife is more precious than gold. (Twi)*

519. *A man is the head of the household, but his wife is its soul. (Ukraine)*

520. *A poor man should only marry one wife, because many wives will cause him trouble. (Turkana)*

521. *A sad bride makes a glad wife. (Holland)*

522. *A smart wife is a great gift from God. (Hungary)*

523. *A wife for a man is as certain as his grave. (Hausa)*

524. *A wife is half an enemy. (Hungary)*

525. *A wife is half helpfulness. (Hungary)*

526. *A wife is not meant to be sent to someone else as a gift. (Twi)*

527. *A wife will hate rice and her husband only momentarily. (Tamil)*

528. *A young wife is for an old man, the horse he rides to hell. (Spain)*

529. *A young wife is poison to an old man. (Sanskrit)*

530. *A young wife, like a mill, always needs adjusting. (Hungary)*

531. *A young wife, new bread, and green wood devastate a house. (Holland)*

532. *An old man's young wife is more cherished than his only son. (Tibet)*

533. *Another's wife is a poisonous plant. (Marathi)*

534. *Another's wife, however pretty, cannot wash your back as your wife can. (Luyia)*

535. *Better to live alone than live with an angry wife. (Oromo)*

536. Between husband and wife only God is a judge. (Yiddish)

537. Choose a wife by your ear rather than by your eye. (Poland)

538. For a young wife her old husband is more boring than a corpse. (Tibet)

539. He is indifferent to his first wife, he is a slave to the later one. (Marathi)

540. He who does not fear for his wife does not love her. (Hungary)

541. He who follows his wife's advice will never see the face of God. (Malta)

542. He who guards his wife has a lot of work. (Hungary)

543. He who wants a wife must look for the bride's looking glass in the kitchen. (Switzerland)

544. If you have five wives, you have five different tongues. (Twi)

545. Is it for beauty's sake that one takes a wife who is useless in time of adversity? (Tamil)

546. Love not only your wife, but her parents too. (Kaonde)

547. Love your wife like a soul; shake her like a pear tree. (Russia)

548. Lying will get you a wife but not keep her. (Fulfulde)

549. Make haste when you are purchasing a field; but when you are to marry a wife be slow. (Hebrew)

550. Ne'er seek a wife till ye ken what to do wi' her. (Scotland)

551. Neither reprove nor flatter your wife where anyone hears or sees it. (Holland)

552. No man is a hero to his wife. (Haya)

553. Old wives are good indeed to wed; the mind is schooled and the stomach fed. (Malaya)

554. One is dear to one's wife as long as one earns and brings it home, but when one is tired and weary, one is dear to one's mother only. (Kashmiri)

555. One is never so desperate as to make one's sister one's wife. (Yoruba)

556. One who does not like his wife finds pebbles in the buttermilk served by her. (Konkani)

557. Only God can bestow a devout wife. (Hungary)

558. *Stale bread is sweet with buttermilk, and a bad wife becomes sweet when she has a child. (Marathi)*

559. *The first wife always controls the co-wives in the household. (Turkana)*

560. *The first wife is mad for her husband; the second wife has something good in her; but the third wife is like an ax on the head. (Kashmiri)*

561. *The first wife is matrimony, the second company, the third heresy. (Poland)*

562. *The wife is the key of the house. (France)*

563. *The wife who has eaten breakfast does not think of her husband's hunger. (Telugu)*

564. *Three things drive a man out of his house: smoke, rain, and a scolding wife. (Poland)*

565. *To have three wives you need three tongues. (Luyia)*

566. *Too many wives cause poverty, but it doesn't matter. (Twi)*

567. *Wealth begins with a wife. (Ukraine)*

568. *Who has a bad wife, his hell begins in earth. (Holland)*

569. *Who is tired of happy days, let him take a wife. (Holland)*

570. *Wives must be had be they good or bad. (Kannada)*

571. *Your first wife is like a mother. (Swahili)*

HUSBAND

572. *A husband is never too shy that he can't speak to his wife. (Yoruba)*

573. *A husband is the ornament of women. (Sanskrit)*

574. *A husband who begs is better than a son who rules over a village. (Telugu)*

575. *Before the bride comes of age the husband will die. (Tamil)*

576. *Chastity means not transgressing a husband's order. (Tamil)*

The wife is the key of the house. (France)

577. *For a husband who eats twelve measures of rice, there is a wife who eats thirteen measures. (Konkani)*

578. *For the husband who does not love his wife there is not enough salt in the Ilakura. (Telugu)*

579. *In the husband wisdom, in the wife gentleness. (England)*

580. *It is an ill husband who is not missed. (Russia)*

581. *My husband has not controlled me, yet my lover runs after me with a club. (Egypt)*

582. *She spoke affectionately with her neighbor, and beat her own husband. (Tamil)*

583. *The husband is the head, the wife the crown on it. (Slovakia)*

584. *The husband is the life of the woman. (Marathi)*

585. *The young brother-in-law is preferred to the husband. (Hausa)*

MARRIAGE & MARRIED LIFE

586. *A bumpy marriage rarely ends well. (Hungary)*

587. *A discussion about marriage has no end. (Hungary)*

588. *A forced marriage doesn't bear good fruit. (Hungary)*

589. *A happy marriage results from a betrothal in a former state of existence. (China)*

590. *A marriage in the house is a fine thing for the village dogs. (Telugu)*

591. *A new marriage picks out the good yam. (Twi)*

592. *A polygamist suffers a lot. (Haya)*

593. *A quarrel between a man and wife only lasts as long as a Pesara seed stays on a looking glass. (Telugu)*

594. *A shotgun marriage won't last longer than the honeymoon. (United States)*

595. *A wedding is bliss. (Swahili)*

596. A young man popular with the girls does not marry; old men do. (Zulu)

597. An unmarried person in Turkanaland is called a fool. (Turkana)

598. Better marry than burn. (Ireland)

599. By day they are ready to divorce, by night they are ready for bed. (Yiddish)

600. By the time the wedding occurs your broken heart will be healed. (Ukraine)

601. Choose your love, then love your choice. (United States)

602. Conversation is like making love; the man is the question, the woman the answer, and the union of both will bear fruit. (Egypt)

603. Court abroad but marry at home. (Ireland)

604. Dressing up doesn't mean marrying girls—otherwise the red finch would have snapped up all the girls on earth. (Luganda)

605. Even though the teeth and the tongue live together they cut each other. (Dagari)

606. For a marriage to be good there must be children. (Kaonde)

607. From bad matches good children are also born. (Yiddish)

608. Getting married takes an hour, but for a whole lifetime one has troubles. (Yiddish)

609. Give your daughter in marriage into a rich family, but get a daughter-in-law from a poor one. (Konkani)

610. He that tells his wife news is but newly married. (England)

611. He who marries a cousin dies in war. (Swahili)

612. He who marries beauty marries trouble. (Yoruba)

613. He who marries two is either a merchant or a wanton. (Egypt)

614. Husband and wife are like one flesh. (Yiddish)

615. Husband and wife are one flesh but they possess two separate pockets. (Yiddish)

616. Husband and wife in perfect concord are like the music of the harp and the lute. (China)

Husband and wife in perfect concord are like the music of the harp and the lute. (China)

617. *Husband and wife must be loyal to one another. (Kaonde)*

618. *Husband and wife, shout and fight, but the pillow brings them together. (Ukraine)*

619. *In the old days we knew nothing about love, but we managed anyway. (Finland)*

620. *It is a sad house where the hen crows louder than the cock. (Poland)*

621. *It's better to break off an engagement than to cancel a marriage contract. (Yiddish)*

622. *It's never too late to die or get married. (Yiddish)*

623. *Keep both eyes open before you are married and afterwards close only one. (Jamaica)*

624. *Keep your eyes wide open before marriage and half shut afterwards. (Russia)*

625. *Like blood, like good, and like age make the happiest marriage. (Poland)*

626. *Living together is possible only after many a confrontation. (Dagari)*

627. *Love comes after marriage. (Iceland)*

628. *Love does wonders, but money makes marriages. (France)*

629. *Love has its own language, but marriage falls back on local dialect. (Russia)*

630. *Love in betrothal never lasts in wedlock. (Haya)*

631. *Marriage and hanging go by destiny. (United States)*

632. *Marriage does not mean repaying one in kind. (Hungary)*

633. *Marriage has teeth and it bites hard. (Jamaica)*

634. *Marriage is a covered dish. (Switzerland)*

635. *Marriage is a game best played by two winners. (Russia)*

636. *Marriage is a lick of honey and a barrel of bitter. (Malta)*

637. *Marriage is a quick solution to more problems. (United States)*

638. *Marriage is both heaven and hell. (Poland)*

639. *Marriage is like a besieged fortress: those who are outside want to come in, and those already in want to be out. (Saudi Arabia)*

640. *Marriage is like a tub of water: after a while it is not so hot. (United States)*

641. *Marriage is not a tight knot but a slipknot. (Madagascar)*

642. *Marriage is not divined for. (Zulu)*

643. *Marriage is slavery, widowhood is salvation, virginity is nobility. (Hungary)*

644. *Marriage is the only evil that men pray for. (Greece)*

645. *Marriage is the only war where you sleep with the enemy. (Mexico)*

646. *Marriage without good faith is like a teapot without a tray. (Morocco)*

647. *Marriage without lovemaking means sad consequences and sorrow. (Malta)*

648. *Marriages, commanders, and kings are God's business. (Hungary)*

649. *Married couples who love each other tell each other a thousand things without talking. (China)*

650. *Marry a man older than you, and not a younger man who will tire of you. (Malta)*

651. *Marry a mountain woman and you will marry the mountain. (Ireland)*

652. *Marry and see for yourself. (Luyia)*

653. *Marry too many times and you'll end up with a eunuch. (Oromo)*

654. *Marry with your ears, not your eyes. (Serbia)*

655. *Matrimony is a school in which one learns too late. (Russia)*

656. *May the borsch be meatless as long as I share it with my sweet mate. (Ukraine)*

657. *Men are April when they woo, December when they wed. (England)*

658. *Nobody knows the secrets that exist between a husband and a wife. (Twi)*

659. *Not all who make love make marriages. (Russia)*

660. *Old men, when they marry young women, make much of death. (Poland)*

661. *One should not think about it too much when marrying or taking pills. (Holland)*

Married couples who love each other tell each other a thousand things without talking. (China)

662. Only someone without experience calls marriage "love." (Luganda)

663. Poverty makes you marry a widow. (Dari)

664. Seduce and you will marry. (Luyia)

665. She who is born beautiful is born married. (Hindi)

666. Shy semen won't give birth. (Nembe)

667. The bachelors crave to get married, and the married ones regret why they got married. (Kashmiri)

668. The first time a girl marries, she consults her parents' wishes; the second time, her own. (China)

669. The girl adored by many will not get married. (Oromo)

670. The man who lunches and marries early will never regret either. (Serbia)

671. The miserable fellow is ruined by his wretched marriage. (Telugu)

672. The monk gets married to please his friend. (Albania)

673. The old coupled with the young never agree. (Poland)

674. The old man's habit, his old woman knows. (Tibet)

675. The quarrel between a husband and wife is like the monsoon rains (which does not last long). (Kashmiri)

676. The woman who loves her husband corrects his faults; the man who loves his wife exaggerates them. (Armenia)

677. There are three things that have to be done quickly: burying the dead, opening the door for a stranger, and fixing your daughter's wedding. (Iran)

678. There is no feast till a roast and no torment till a marriage. (Ireland)

679. Those who had some relation in a former state of being are united in marriage in the present life. (China)

680. Though she be ugly as a monkey, marry a girl of your own caste. (Tamil)

681. To marry is to throw oneself away. (Zulu)

682. To marry once is a duty, twice a folly, and three times—madness. (Holland)

The old man's habit, his old woman knows. (Tibet)

683. *To understand your parents' love you must raise children yourself. (China)*

684. *Two people are better than one. (Haya)*

685. *Virginity can be put to only one test. (Hungary)*

686. *Wedding day, bountiful day: then there is no sick woman I say. (Hungary)*

687. *Wedlock, a padlock. (England)*

688. *Who has a scold, has sorrow to his sops. (Poland)*

689. *Who marries for love without money, has good nights and sorry days. (England)*

690. *Who weds for love, has good nights and bad days. (Germany)*

691. *Woe to the house where the hen crows and the rooster keeps still. (Spain)*

692. *You don't divorce someone who rides horses and then marry someone who walks on foot. (Yoruba)*

693. *Young girls dream of marriage, married women dream of love. (Italy)*

WHEN, WHERE, & IF

694. *When a woman weds she obeys her husband; when she is old she obeys her children. (Japan)*

695. *When an old man takes a young wife, he become young and she old. (Yiddish)*

696. *When four eyes met then love came to the heart. (Hindi)*

697. *When husband and wife live in harmony, they can dry up the ocean without a bucket. (Vietnam)*

698. *When love flees it is futile to pursue it. (Italy)*

699. *When love has fallen apart there is no glue strong enough to hold it together. (Italy)*

700. *When love hurts, only death will cure. (Poland)*

Young girls dream of marriage, married women dream of love.
(Italy)

701. When love is greatest, words are fewest. *(United States)*

702. When love is not madness, it is not love. *(Spain)*

703. When love is torn apart one cannot gather the pieces. *(France)*

704. When love sets the table food tastes best. *(England)*

705. When one is in love one begins to deceive oneself and ends by deceiving others. *(Italy)*

706. When one is in love, a cliff becomes a meadow. *(Ethiopia)*

707. When one tries to hide love, one gives the best evidence of its existence. *(Italy)*

708. When passionately in love, one becomes stupid. *(Japan)*

709. When poverty enters the door, love goes out the window. *(Italy)*

710. When talking about love, there can't be talk about sacrifice. *(Czech Republic)*

711. When the bride is expecting, the wedding guests look away. *(Yiddish)*

712. When the coquette flirts with charm even the clay idol breaks out in smiles. *(Tibet)*

713. When the heart is full, the eyes overflow. *(Yiddish)*

714. When the husband and wife live in harmony, the welfare of the family will be secure. *(China)*

715. When the husband earns well the wife spins well. *(Holland)*

716. When the husband is a coachman, he is not afraid of his wife's curses. *(Yiddish)*

717. When the wife is a queen, the husband is a king. *(Yiddish)*

718. When there is marriage without love, there will be love without marriage. *(France)*

719. When two are in love, only one needs to eat. *(Spain)*

720. When you have a pretty wife, you are a bad friend. *(Yiddish)*

721. When you look for a woman, do not read her by her face. *(Malta)*

722. When you love someone don't let him know it. *(Malta)*

723. When you love, love the moon; when you steal, steal a camel. *(Egypt)*

When the coquette flirts with charm even the clay idol breaks out in smiles. (Tibet)

724. When your destined spouse appears, you'll know it when you hear the first few spoken words. (Yiddish)

725. Where distrust enters, love is no more than a pageboy. (Chile)

726. Where the heart is, there is happiness. (Iran)

727. Where the heart loves, there the legs walk. (Malta)

728. Where the wife is a queen, the husband is a king. (Yiddish)

729. Where there is a husband of stone there is a paramour. (Marathi)

730. Where there is least heart there is most speech. (Montnegro)

731. Where there is love all things are done well. (Spain)

732. Where there is love it never feels crowded. (Yiddish)

733. Where there is love, there is faith. (Latin)

734. Where there is no love, all faults are seen. (Russia)

735. Where you sow love, joy grows. (Germany)

736. If love is the sickness then patience is the remedy. (Hausa)

737. If a husband is unfaithful, it is like spitting from the house to the street; but if a wife is unfaithful, it is like spitting from the street into the house. (Russia)

738. If a woman has a faithful husband and a little rice, she may make her domestic happiness as beautiful as a picture. (Tamil)

739. If one girl dislikes you, take up with another. (Hausa)

740. If one loves one's wife, then one loves her family too. (Yiddish)

741. If someone says, "There's a wedding in the clouds," then the women would soon arrive with their ladders. (Saudi Arabia)

742. If the bride can't dance, she claims the musicians can't play. (Yiddish)

743. If the bride has no horse to ride then spare her carrying the pots and pans. (Fulfulde)

744. If the heart is not in it the words will fool no one. (Ukraine)

745. If the husband has no property, even his own wife will not respect him. (Tamil)

746. If a man lets a woman know what he has got in his savings, she will marry him for his money. (Malta)

747. *If there is love the impossible becomes possible. (Tamil)*

748. *If there is no food for one day, a father's love grows cold; if there is no food for three days, a wife's love grows cold. (China)*

749. *If there's a beautiful woman around, she'll soon smoke out the adulterers. (Kaonde)*

750. *If two married people love each other, they will avoid much sorrow. (Swahili)*

751. *If you cheat your wife sooner or later she'll find out. (Kaonde)*

752. *If you give a girl away in marriage with one hand, ten hands will not bring her back. (Yoruba)*

753. *If you had one bad marriage in a village, don't go there looking for another wife. (Kaonde)*

754. *If you have no relatives, get married. (Egypt)*

755. *If you live in love and harmony you don't even need a treasury. (Russia)*

756. *If you love a lot love also a little. (Russia)*

757. *If you love an ugly person, you make them beautiful. (Luganda)*

758. *If you love me do not forget me; if you do not, do not mention me. (Ukraine)*

759. *If you marry early, you will regret it early. (Hungary)*

760. *If you marry your daughter into a great house a visit to her will be a rarity. (Marathi)*

761. *If you possess something you will be loved; if you have nothing, even the dog will be better respected. (Hausa)*

762. *If you think Miss this-year is pretty, Miss next-year will be more so. (Hausa)*

763. *If you're faithful to your wife, you'll have a healthy body. (Yiddish)*

NATIONS, REGIONS, AND LANGUAGES
REPRESENTED IN
TREASURY OF LOVE PROVERBS
FROM MANY LANDS

NATIONS

1. ALBANIA	31. JAMAICA
2. ARGENTINA	32. JAPAN
3. ARMENIA	33. LATVIA
4. BELGIUM	34. LEBANON
5. BRAZIL	35. LITHUANIA
6. BULGARIA	36. MADAGASCAR
7. CAMBODIA	37. MALTA
8. CANADA	38. MEXICO
9. CHILE	39. MOROCCO
10. CHINA	40. MYANMAR
11. CONGO	41. NORWAY
12. CUBA	42. PHILIPPINES
13. CZECH REPUBLIC	43. POLAND
14. DENMARK	44. PORTUGAL

15. EGYPT	45. ROMANIA
16. ENGLAND	46. RUSSIA
17. ESTONIA	47. SAUDI ARABIA
18. ETHIOPIA	48. SCOTLAND
19. FINLAND	49. SERBIA
20. FRANCE	50. SLOVAKIA
21. GEORGIA	51. SLOVENIA
22. GERMANY	52. SPAIN
23. GREECE	53. SUDAN
24. GUINEA	54. SWEDEN
25. HOLLAND	55. SWITZERLAND
26. HUNGARY	56. TURKEY
27. ICELAND	57. UKRAINE
28. IRAN	58. UNITED STATES
29. IRELAND	59. VIETNAM
30. ITALY	60. WALES

REGIONS

61. ISLE OF MAN	63. MONTENEGRO
62. KURDISTAN	64. TIBET

LANGUAGES

65. BASQUE	83. MAORI
66. DAGARI	84. MARATHI
67. DARI	85. MASAI
68. FULFULDE	86. NEMBE
69. HAUSA	87. OROMO
70. HAWAIIAN	88. SANSKRIT
71. HAYA	89. SHONA
72. HEBREW	90. SWAHILI
73. HINDI	91. TAMIL
74. IGBO	92. TELUGU
75. KANNADA	93. TSONGA
76. KAONDE	94. TURKANA
77. KASHMIRI	95. TWI
78. KONKANI	96. WOLOF

79. LATIN

80. LUGANDA

81. LUYIA

82. MALAY

97. YAKA

98. YIDDISH

99. YORUBA

100. ZULU

Children's love is like water in a basket. (Argentina)

ALBANIA

Love is sometimes difficult but death even more so.
The monk gets married to please his friend.

ARGENTINA

Children's love is like water in a basket.

ARMENIA

Every man has three ears: one on the left of his head, one on the
right, and one in his heart.
The woman who loves her husband corrects his faults; the man who
loves his wife exaggerates them.

BASQUE

Satisfy a dog with a bone; a woman with a lie.

BELGIUM

Love that blushes is a flower; love that pales, a tragedy of the heart.

BRAZIL

Love is blind, that's why you have to touch.

BULGARIA

Stronger even than stone is a man's heart.

CAMBODIA

Cultivate a heart of love that knows no anger.
Don't shoot those you hate, and don't lend to those you love.

CANADA

Every heart has its own ache.
Great love from little things may grow.
Love goes where it's sent.
Old love is easily kindled.
The heart that loves is always young.
They love too much that die for love.
True love never runs smooth.

CHILE

Where distrust enters, love is no more than a pageboy.

CHINA

A happy marriage results from a betrothal in a former state of exist-
ence.
A hero cannot get out of the influence of women.
Affection is like glue or varnish.
Estrangement springs from jealousy.
Husband and wife in perfect concord are like the music of the harp
and the lute.
If there is no food for one day, a father's love grows cold; if there is
no food for three days, a wife's love grows cold.
In sickness of the heart, it is the medicine of love that can affect a
cure.
Married couples who love each other tell each other a thousand
things without talking.
Tenderness causes love and love causes doltishness.
The first time a girl marries, she consults her parents' wishes; the sec-
ond time, her own.
The heart is but the beach beside the sea that is the world
There is no cure for jealousy.
Those who had some relation in a former state of being are united in
marriage in the present life.
Time reveals a man's heart.
To understand your parents' love you must raise children yourself.
When the heart is at ease, the body is healthy.
When the husband and wife live in harmony, the welfare of the fam-
ily will be secure.

CONGO

Love is like a baby: it needs to be treated tenderly.
Lovers do not hide their nakedness.
To love someone who does not love you is like shaking a tree to make the dew drops fall.
Woe to the high-spirited bride whose mother-in-law is still alive.

CUBA

A pain in the bone is better than a pain in the heart.
That which does not go away in tears, goes away in sighs.

CZECH REPUBLIC

Even if man would be fully satisfied with everything else, he will always crave more love.
Hate calls for disputes, love conquers all offenses.
Like a face reflecting itself in water, so does man reflect his heart.
Love can't be begged for, nor threatened for.
Love is a disease, but it does not want to be healed.
When talking about love, there can't be talk about sacrifice.

DAGARI (Burkina Faso)

A bachelor should not woo a woman for another man.
Even though the teeth and the tongue live together they cut each other.

Living together is possible only after many a confrontation.

DARI (Chad)

Poverty makes you marry a widow.

DENMARK

Faults are thick where love is thin.
Love is blind and thinks others don't see either.
Love is one-eyed; hate is blind.
Love produces heroes, but also idiots.

EGYPT

Conversation is like making love; the man is the question, the
woman the answer, and the union of both will bear fruit.
He who marries two is either a merchant or a wanton.
If you have no relatives, get married.
Love and let everyone know; hate and be silent.
My husband has not controlled me, yet my lover runs after me with
a club.
When you love, love the moon; when you steal, steal a camel.

ENGLAND

A kiss of the mouth often touches not the heart.
A lisping lass is good to kiss.
Better to be an old man's sweetheart than a young man's slave.
Happy is the wooing that is not long in doing.
He that tells his wife news is but newly married.
In the husband wisdom, in the wife gentleness.
Love delights in praise.
Love laughs at locksmiths.
Love lives in cottages as well as in courts.
Love will creep where it cannot go.
Men are April when they woo, December when they wed.
They love too much that die for love.
Wedlock, a padlock.
Who marries for love without money, has good nights and sorry
days.

ESTONIA

Love makes cottages manors; straw, silken ribbons.
The mouth is the interpreter of the heart.

ETHIOPIA

When one is in love, a cliff becomes a meadow.

Love deprives the wise of half their wit, fools of everything.
(Finland)

FINLAND

At birth love is blind like a kitten, but as it grows older it receives a
hundred eyes.
Even horses kick when in love.
Hugging does not cure desire.
Love blinds your eyes, marriage opens them wide.
Love deprives the wise of half their wit, fools of everything.
Love does not measure distance.
Love is a flower garden and marriage is a field of nettles.
Love is severe and devotion tough, it kills you on your feet and the
eyes remain open.
Love pulls as hard as five teams of oxen.
The love of one's youth and Christmas cheese will always be remem-
bered.

FRANCE

A love defined is a love that is finished.
Being loved is the best way of being useful.
First love letters are written with the eye.
In love there is always one who kisses and one who offers the cheek.
Love brings the distant near.
Love does wonders, but money makes marriages.
Love endures many delays.
Love engenders love.
Love is often the fruit of marriage.
Love is the longing to achieve another's happiness by achieving our
own.
Love makes time pass; time makes love pass.
Love never dies of starvation, but often of indigestion.
Love teaches even donkeys to dance.
Love, your pains are worth more than all other pleasures combined.
Loving with the eyes only, has blinded a lot of fools.

One always returns to one's first love.
One lover, that is love; two lovers, that is passion; three lovers, that is commerce.
Real love is when you don't have to tell each other.
The end of passion is the beginning of repentance.
The love that you die from is too big.
The torch of love is lit in the kitchen.
The wife is the key of the house.
There is no such thing as nice prisons and ugly loves.
Try to reason about love and you will lose your reason.
When there is marriage without love, there will be love without marriage.
When we cannot get what we love, we must love what is within our reach.

FULFULDE (West Africa)

If the bride has no horse to ride than spare her carrying the pots and pans.
Lying will get you a wife but not keep her.
Your hypocrisy is like that of a woman who carries her husband and her co-wife on her back.

GEORGIA

Great love is followed by great hate.

GERMANY

A woman can't drive her husband, but she can lead him.
Forced love and painted cheeks don't last.
Jealousy is a pain that eagerly seeks what causes pain.
Love at a distance stays warm the longest.
Love at first sight is often extinguished by the second.
Love at first sight is the most common eye disease.
Love creates love in response
Love fills the world and multiplies heaven.
Love is blinding. That is why lovers like to touch.
Love is the beginning of sorrow.
Love knows hidden paths.
Love needs quarrel.
Love will creep where it may not go.
Love without reciprocity is a question without an answer.
Old love does not rust.
Smart women love foolish men.
Straw in your shoe and love in your heart will always show.
The lover who hurts is the only one who can heal.
Where you sow love, joy grows.
Who weds for love, has good nights and bad days.

GREECE

Marriage is the only evil that men pray for.
The heart that loves is always young.

GUINEA

For news of the heart ask the face.

HAUSA (Nigeria, Niger)

A love match without means of support recoils on the makers.
A man no longer married is more dangerous than one not yet married.
A wife for a man is as certain as his grave.
A woman who admits she is in the wrong won't want for a husband.
Getting engaged is not hard, paying the money is.
He who deserts his household will be deserted by them.
If love is the sickness then patience is the remedy.
If one girl dislikes you, take up with another.
If you possess something you will be loved; if you have nothing,
even the dog will be better respected.
If you think Miss this-year is pretty, Miss next-year will be more so.
Loving one who loves another is a bellyful of trouble.
The handsome man is king , if there is no rich man near.
The young brother-in-law is preferred to the husband.

HAWAIAN

Love is like fog, there is no mountain on which it does not rest.

HAYA (Tanzania)

A polygamist suffers a lot.
Love in betrothal never lasts in wedlock.
No man is a hero to his wife.
The one you love is always wished success.
Two people are better than one.

HEBREW

Love is a sweet dream and marriage is the alarm clock.
Make haste when you are purchasing a field; but when you are to
marry a wife be slow.

HINDI

She who is born beautiful is born married.
The hand to the nail and the heart to the beloved.
When four eyes met then love came to the heart.

HOLLAND

A kiss without a beard is like an egg without salt.
A sad bride makes a glad wife.
A young wife, new bread, and green wood devastate a house.
Forced love does not last.
He that has luck leads the bride to church.
Love makes labor light.
Neither reprove nor flatter your wife where anyone hears or sees it.
Nobody's sweetheart is ugly.
One should not think about it too much when marrying or taking
pills.
Out of the abundance of the heart the mouth speaks.
The heart does not lie.
To marry once is a duty, twice a folly, and three times—madness.
When the husband earns well the wife spins well.
Who has a bad wife, his hell begins in earth.
Who is tired of happy days, let him take a wife.
Who writes love letters grows thin; who carries them, fat.

When the husband earns well the wife spins well. (Holland)

HUNGARY

A bumpy marriage rarely ends well.
A discussion about marriage has no end.
A forced marriage doesn't bear good fruit.
A smart wife is a great gift from God.
A spinster is like an old letter that was written, and was never sent.
A wife is half an enemy.
A wife is half helpfulness.
A young wife, like a mill, always needs adjusting.
Any old woman, if she marries, is a bride.
He who does not fear for his wife dies not love her.
He who guards his wife has a lot of work.
If you marry early, you will regret it early.
It's a pitiful kiss, if you have to pay for it.
Kisses are not for nothing.
Love and anger are not fair judges.
Love and the nobility don't tolerate sharing.
Love is cunning, it wears golden fetters.
Love, smoke, and coughing cannot be hidden.
Love, wine, and gambling empty the purse.
Marriage does not mean repaying one in kind.
Marriage is slavery, widowhood is salvation, virginity is nobility.
Marriages, commanders, and kings are God's business.
Only God can bestow a devout wife.
Virginity can be put to only one test.
Wedding day, bountiful day: then there is no sick woman I say.

ICELAND

Love comes after marriage.

IGBO (Nigeria)

He who waits for his lover hears the footsteps of the spirits.
Just because my girlfriend is beautiful, it doesn't mean I'll climb a
pear tree protected with charms.

IRAN

A broken hand works, but not a broken heart.
Allah gives to us according to the measure of our hearts.
Don't just take love, experience it.
He whose heart is arouse by love will never die.
Only a heart can find the way to another heart.
Persian was the language of love spoken by Adam and Eve, but the
angel that took them away from Paradise spoke Turkish.
Rose water is not for the backs of old folk, but for the breasts of
young lovers.
The lover who gives you her body but not her heart is generous with
thornless roses.
There are three things that have to be done quickly: burying the
dead, opening the door for a stranger, and fixing your daughter's
wedding.
Where the heart is, there is happiness.

IRELAND

Better marry than burn.
Court abroad but marry at home.
It is a lonesome washing without a man's shirt in it.
Marry a mountain woman and you will marry the mountain.
There is no feast till a roast and no torment till a marriage.

ISLE OF MAN

A kind heart is better than a crafty head.

ITALY

A man without a woman is a tree without leaves and branches.
A quarrel is the renewing of love.
A silent passion increases more ardently.
A woman's fate is determined by the love she accepts.
Declarations of a woman's love should be written in water and her
promises scribbled in the sand.
Fear and love never go together.
For women, there is no good in life except love.
In her first passion woman loves her lover, in all others she is in love
with love.
In the war of love, the one who flees wins.
It is best to love wisely, no doubt, but to love foolishly is better than
not to love at all.
Jealousy can be as cruel as death.
Love and mastery are not companions.
Love begins with song and dance and ends in a sea of tears.
Love conceals all of one's faults.
Love does much; money does everything.
Love is a blind guide and those who follow him often lose their way.
Love is blind and cannot see the pretty follies which lovers them-
selves commit.
Love is blind but can see far away.
Love is blind but marriage restores one's vision.
Love is born by curiosity, endures by habit.
Love is never without troubles.
Love is nourished by mutual sacrifice.
Love is often bitter, but it reassures the heart.

Without wine and food even love grows pale. (Italy)

Love is only a portion of a man's life, but it is the whole of a woman's life.
Love no longer lives when hope is dead.
Love perceives nothing as labor.
Love rules his kingdom without a sword.
Love rules without any laws.
Love without strife is love that is smoldering.
New loves come and go, an old love remains.
Not to have been loved is a misfortune, but not to have loved is a tragedy.
Old loves are never forgotten.
One cannot hide love from a lover's eyes.
One cannot make laws to rule the heart. The power of love cannot be compelled.
One who tries to unite prudence and love knows nothing about love.
One who wants to be a lover must be brave.
Perfect love casts out all fears.
The anger of lovers lasts a short time.
The crowning moment of our life, happiness without peace, this is love.
The language of love is in the eyes.
The magic of the first love is the ignorance that it can never end.
The only merit of a man is his good sense, but the greatest merit of a woman is her beauty.
The power of love is determined by the strength the heart has given to it.
The result of love is jealousy and broken faith.
The sound of a kiss is not as strong as that of a canon but its echo may endure much longer.
The weather is always fair when people are in love.
There is no love so true as one which dies untold.
There is nothing in the world as sweet as love.
To tell the truth, love and reason are seldom seen in the same company.
True love can never become old.
True paradise is not in the heavens but upon the mouth of a woman in love.

When love flees it is futile to pursue it.
When love has fallen apart there is no glue strong enough to hold it together.
When one is in love one begins to deceive oneself and ends by deceiving others.
When one tries to hide love, one gives the best evidence of its existence.
When poverty enters the door, love goes out the window.
Without wine and food even love grows pale.
You will not be loved if you think yourself alone.
Young girls dream of marriage, married women dream of love.

JAMAICA

Keep both eyes open before you are married and afterwards close only one.
Marriage has teeth and it bites hard.

JAPAN

A man in love mistakes a harelip for a dimple.
A man's heart changes as often as does the autumn sky.
Eating comes before being in love.
He who treads the path of love walks a thousand meters as if it were only one.
If you make love in the shade you get cold.
Jealousy is the life of love.
Love knows no difference between high and low.
The human heart is neither of stone nor wood.
Two lovers in the rain have no need of an umbrella.

When a woman weds she obeys her husband; when she is old she
obeys her children.
When passionately in love, one becomes stupid.

KANNADA (Southwestern India)

A man's best fortune or his worst is his wife.
Wives must be had be they good or bad.

KAONDE (Zambia)

A woman cannot be proud of her husband unless he gives her chil-
dren.
For a marriage to be good there must be children.
Husband and wife must be loyal to one another.
If there's a beautiful woman around, she'll soon smoke out the adul-
terers.
If you cheat your wife sooner or later she'll find out.
If you had one bad marriage in a village, don't go there looking for
another wife.
Love not only your wife, but her parents too.

KASHMIRI (Kashmir)

A blind man's wife is God's keeping.
A good wife is a blessing, and a bad one is a curse.
A pampered girl may not get a husband of her choice.
Neither do I want honey nor the sting of the bee.

One is dear to one's wife as long as one earns and brings it home,
but when one is tired and weary, one is dear to one's mother only.
One woman is like a hundred-branched maple tree to you, another is
like a bitch at the door.
The bachelors crave to get married, and the married ones regret why
they got married.
The first wife is mad for her husband; the second wife has some-
thing good in her; but the third wife is like an ax on the head.
The quarrel between a husband and wife is like the monsoon rains
(which does not last long).

KONKANI (Western India)

For a husband who eats twelve measures of rice, there is a wife who
eats thirteen measures.
Give your daughter in marriage into a rich family, but get a daugh-
ter-in-law from a poor one.
One who does not like his wife finds pebbles in the buttermilk
served by her.
The bride's culture can be judged by her conduct at the marriage
ceremony.
The bridegroom strong and healthy and the bride tender and sweet,
make a good match.

KURDISTAN

He who loves a woman is a nephew of the sun.
If you cannot build a town, build a heart.

LATIN

A shameful love is usually deaf.
He who does not love does not strive.
Love and a cough cannot be hidden.
Love and fear exclude each other.
Love if you want to be loved.
Pretense of love is worse than hatred.
To love is to deny oneself.
Tomorrow shall be love for the loveless and for the lover tomorrow shall be love.
Where there is love, there is faith.

LATVIA

Love and fear never go together.

LEBANON

Love blinds itself to all shortcomings.

LITHUANIA

With eyes you will win love.

LUGANDA (Uganda)

A lover who loves you not is like the calf of your leg which turns its back on whatever side your stomach turns to.
A man afraid to join the army and a lazy woman are made for each other.
Dressing up doesn't mean marrying girls—otherwise the red finch would have snapped up all the girls on earth.
If you love an ugly person, you make them beautiful.
Love consumes understanding.
"No more joy," you say when the one you love goes to war.
"No more trouble," you say when the one you love arrives.
Only someone without experience calls marriage "love."
Poverty does not let you know the one who might love you.
The extent of my love for you is buried in stone.
Those in love need only the smallest of places.
You'd even build your house on a hard rock for someone who loves you.

LUYIA (Kenya)

A bride's eyes pretend not to see.
A woman who moves from husband to husband has no manners.
Another's wife, however pretty, cannot wash your back as your wife can.
Do not be put off by a partner's poor dancing.
Don't believe in pillow talk.
Marry and see for yourself.
Seduce and you will marry.
The heart desires that which is out of reach.
To have three wives you need three tongues.

Those in love need only the smallest of places. (Luganda)

MADAGASCAR

A good wife is easy to find, but suitable in-laws are rare.
Don't be so much in love that you can't tell when it's raining.
Let your love be like drizzle: it comes softly, but still swells the river.
Love is like rice; if you plant it elsewhere it will also grow.
Marriage is not a tight knot but a slipknot.

MALAY (Malaysia)

Old wives are good indeed to wed; the mind is schooled and the
stomach fed.

MALTA

A kiss without a hug is like a flower without a fragrance.
A lovely girl attracts attention by her good looks, an ugly girl by the
help of a mirror.
A man who makes a fool of himself on account of a woman is done
for.
At night all women are alike.
Carnal love is stronger than sacramental love.
Far from the eye, far from the heart.
For every ugly man there are a pair of foolish eyes.
He who follows his wife's advice will never see the face of God.
He who loves you brings you joy, but in the end he will make you
cry.
He who loves you is worth loving.
If a man lets a woman know what he has got in his savings, she will
marry him for his money.
Kisses are like almonds.

Love has no light, pity has no rays.
Love is the sister of madness.
Marriage is a lick of honey and a barrel of bitter.
Marriage without love-making means sad consequences and sorrow.
Marry a man older than you, and not a younger man who will tire of you.
One does not notice the faults of the person one loves.
The good looks of a woman are her dowry.
Whatever a bride touches is fragrant.
When you look for a woman, do not read her by her face.
When you love someone don't let him know it.
Where the heart loves, there the legs walk.
Your mistress's visit brings you good luck.

MAORI (New Zealand)

You can peek into houses but not hearts.

MARATHI (Western India)

An impatient bridegroom ties the head ornaments to his knees.
Another's wife is a poisonous plant.
He is indifferent to the first wife, he is a slave to the later one.
If you marry your daughter into a great house a visit to her will be a rarity.
Stale bread is sweet with buttermilk, and a bad wife becomes sweet when she has a child.
The husband is the life of the woman.
Where there is a husband of stone there is a paramour.

MASAI (Tanzania, Kenya)

Carry on with your lover as you tend your flock.

MEXICO

A jealous lover becomes an indifferent spouse.
Love is blind—but not the neighbors.
Love is too rare to lose to jealousy.
Marriage is the only war where you sleep with the enemy.
No fate is worse than a life without love.
The lover of a student does not always become the wife of a graduate.

MONTENEGRO

Where there is least heart there is most speech.

MOROCCO

Marriage without good faith is like a teapot without a tray.

MYANMAR

It is as difficult to win love as it is to pack salt in pine needles.
The more violent the love, the more violent the anger.

What love is, is peace. (Myanmar)

What love is, is peace.

NEMBE (Nigeria)

Shy semen won't give birth.
The new one is the loved one.

NORWAY

A fair bride needs little finery.
That which is loved is always beautiful.

OROMO (Horn of Africa)

A man with two wives will die of hunger or a curse.
A woman married without her consent runs away without consent.
Better to live alone than live with an angry wife.
Extreme love brings extreme hatred.
I have no desire of husband, said the nine-times married woman.
Just because your lover has come, honey won't turn into mead.
Marry too many times and you'll end up with a eunuch.
No one hates beauty, but beauty hates someone.
The girl adored by many will not get married.
The poor man marries a pregnant woman.
Women say a lover comes while grain is mashing.

PHILIPPINES

Disquiet is the constant companion of jealousy.

POLAND

A faint heart never won a fair lady.
A girl's love, luck in cards, the squire's favor, and the rose's bloom don't last.
A good wife is a goodly prize.
Beauty does not grow love, love grows beauty.
Choose a wife by your ear rather than by your eye.
Hot love is soon cold.
It is a sad house where the hen crows louder than the cock.
Like blood, like good, and like age make the happiest marriage.
Love and lordship like no fellowship.
Love can tear you from a rosary to a dance.
Love feeds without bread.
Love governs the heart, resentments drive the mind.
Love has a long nose.
Love is born of love.
Love is never without jealousy.
Love knows no dangers.
Love lives on hope and dies with it.
Love makes all hard hearts gentle.
Love scorns duty.
Love sweetens everything.
Love without jealousy is like a Pole without a mustache.
Love without money is a gate to misery.
Lucky is he who knew reciprocal love or none at all.
Marriage is both heaven and hell.
Old men, when they marry young women, make much of death.
One cannot love and be wise.
Physical or dishonest love is obscene and damaging.

A girl's love, luck in cards, the squire's favor, and the rose's bloom don't last. (Poland)

The first wife is matrimony, the second company, the third heresy.
The greater the love, the greater the obstacle.
The old coupled with the young never agree.
The way is never long to one's beloved.
Three things drive a man out of his house: smoke, rain, and a scolding wife.
When love hurt, only death will cure.
Who has a scold, has sorrow to his sops.
With hungry people love cannot last long.
You cannot threaten someone to love you.

PORTUGAL

Love does not recognize the law.
Love is like the moon: if it doesn't get bigger, it gets smaller.

ROMANIA

Better an ugly love from your village, than a beauty from an unknown one.
Love understands all languages.
Short love, long sighs.

RUSSIA

All the world loves a lover.
If a husband is unfaithful, it is like spitting from the house to the street; but if a wife is unfaithful, it is like spitting from the street into the house.

If you live in love and harmony you don't even need a treasury.
If you love a lot love also a little.
It is an ill husband who is not missed.
Keep your eyes wide open before marriage and half shut afterwards.
Love and death know no limits.
Love and eggs are best when they are fresh.
Love and smoke cannot be hidden.
Love begins with the eyes.
Love but do not fall in love.
Love does not look but sees everything.
Love has its own language, but marriage falls back on local dialect.
Love is a circle and an endless sphere.
Love is a ring and a ring has no beginning and no end.
Love is heavy, but lack of love is heavier.
Love is like glass that breaks if handled clumsily.
Love is not found in the market.
Love redeems many sins.
Love's strength is truth.
Love your wife like a soul, shake her like a palm tree.
Many are betrayed with a kiss.
Marriage is a game best played by two winners.
Matrimony is a school in which one learns too late.
Not all who make love make marriages.
The heart that loves is always young.
Those who love you will make you weep; those who hate you will
make you laugh.
Where there is no love, all faults are seen.

SANSKRIT

A husband is the ornament of women.
A young wife is poison to an old man.
An old woman, a chaste wife.
As a man's heart is, so does he speak.
In the absence of men all women are chaste.

Take an excellent woman even from a bad caste.
Whom on earth will a handsome woman not subdue?

SAUDI ARABIA

He who loves thinks the others are blind; the others think he is crazy.
If someone says, "There is a wedding in the clouds," then the
women would soon arrive with their ladders.
Love has sharp vision, hate's is sharper, but jealousy's is sharpest be-
cause it combines love and hate.
Love lasts as long as does the reproach.
Love makes a man blind and deaf.
Marriage is like a besieged fortress: those who are outside want to
come in, and those already in want to be out.
There are three things that can never be hidden—love, a mountain,
and one riding on a camel.
To love someone truly you have to love them as if your beloved
were to die tomorrow.
Words from the heart reach the heart, words from the mouth reach
the ear.

SCOTLAND

Faint heart ne'er wan fair lady.
For luve o' the nurse mony ane kisses the bairn.
Ne'er seek a wife till ye ken what to do wi' her.

SERBIA

Marry with your ears, not your eyes.
The man who lunches and marries early will never regret either.

SHONA

A man is attractive when he is not your husband.
Love is like a color which fades away.

SLOVAKIA

A secret love is always a true love.
The heart does not grieve over what the eyes have not seen.
The husband is the head, the wife the crown on it.

SLOVENIA

Love is full of honey and gall.

SPAIN

A nun's love is a raging inferno.
A young wife is for an old man the horse he rides to hell.
He who finds not love finds nothing.

A nun's love is a raging inferno. (Spain)

In love all is sadness; but sadness and all, it's still the best thing in
life.
In the face of love and death courage is useless.
In war, hunting, and love a little pleasure gives a lot of pain.
It's better to eat dry bread in love than a feast in sorrow.
Love can do a lot, money still more.
Love is a bad neighbor, but to have none is worse.
Love is like a mousetrap: you go in when you want, but you don't
get out when you like.
Love is like war: you begin when you like and leave off when you
can.
Love is works not words.
Love kills with golden arrows.
Love, pain, and money cannot be kept secret; they soon betray them-
selves.
Lovers swear that everyone else is blind.
Man is fire, woman dry straw, then the devil comes along and blows.
Mistakes made for love are worthy of forgiveness.
One who truly loves finds it difficult to forget.
The one who truly loves you will cause you pain.
Vows of love and smoke from the fireplace, the wind blows them
both away.
When love is not madness, it is not love.
When two are in love, only one needs to eat.
Where there is love all things are done well.
Woe to the house where the hen crows and the rooster keeps still.
Woman without man is like fire without wood.

SUDAN

The greatness of love obliterates conventions.

SWAHILI (Tanzania, Kenya)

A handsome finger gets a ring put around it.
A letter from the heart can be read on the face.
A lover has no grudge.
A loving heart can also reject.
A loving heart is not to be argued with.
A man if loved, should love.
A pole is not a spear, seduction is not the same as wedlock.
A poor man's love is never seen.
A pretty face needs no adornment.
A wedding is bliss.
An honorable woman doesn't flirt.
For the disease of love there is no cure.
He who loves me, I also love him; he who rejects me diminishes my grief.
He who marries a cousin dies in war.
If two married people love each other, they will avoid much sorrow.
It is not I, it is my heart.
Love has neither eyes nor understanding.
Love is a metal pot: off the fire it cools at once.
Love is only love when it affects both sides.
Love is sweet, love is poison.
Love without gifts does not become evident at all.
Someone in love is drunk.
The gain of love is little, is little.
The heart of a human being is as deep as a well.
The tears of one who loves will come even from a bad eye.
Three things refresh the heart: water, flowers, and a beautiful face.
To give love to one who loves you not is like rain falling on the desert.
Victory makes a man popular, and to fall in love means to be conquered.
You cannot bring back love or life.
You know sweetness can kill, so why have you given me poison?
Your first wife is like a mother.

SWEDEN

A life without love is like a year without summer.
Love brings forth many heroes, but even more idiots.

SWITZERLAND

He who wants a wife must look for the bride's looking glass in the
kitchen.
Marriage is a covered dish.

TAMIL (Southern India, Sri Lanka, Malaysia)

A character full of love is like a river without a wave.
A wife will hate rice and her husband only momentarily.
Beauty without chastity is a flower without smell.
Before the bride comes of age the husband will die.
Chastity means not transgressing a husband's order.
He who is not melted by anything else may be melted by love.
If a woman has a faithful husband and a little rice, she may make her
domestic happiness as beautiful as a picture.
If the husband has no property, even his own wife will not respect
him.
If there is love the impossible becomes possible.
Is it for beauty's sake that one takes a wife who is useless in time of
adversity?
It is better to throw oneself into a well than to marry an old man.
She spoke affectionately with her neighbor, and beat her own hus-
band.
The heart is its own witness.
Though she be ugly as a monkey, marry a girl of your own caste.

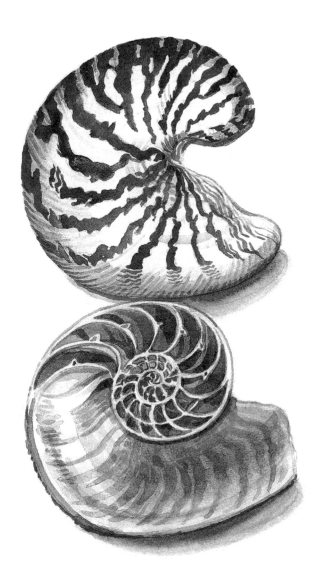

It's love that makes the seashell stick to the rock. (Twi)

Though your friendship reach her bosom, don't put your hand on her bosom.

TELUGU (Southeastern India)

A helpless woman will get a foolish husband.
A husband who begs is better than a son who rules over a village.
A marriage in the house is a fine thing for the village dogs.
A quarrel between a man and wife only lasts as long as a Pesara seed stays on a looking glass.
Even the goddess of pestilence passes over the woman unloved by her husband.
For the husband who does not love his wife there is not enough salt in the Ilakura.
The daughter-in-law enters the house [as a bride], and the mother-in-law enters the Ganges [dies].
The miserable fellow is ruined by his wretched marriage.
The wife who has eaten breakfast does not think of her husband's hunger.

TIBET

A woman without jewelry is a plain nun.
Affection that is genuine never turns a heart into a stone.
Amorality and virtue are hard to distinguish.
An old man's young wife is more cherished than his only son.
Divorced women know no constant companion.
For a young wife her old husband is more boring than a corpse.
Infatuation is faster than a horse with a tail shorter than a sheep's.
It's an inexperienced man who marries a barren woman.
Men may look alike but their hearts differ.
On the cliff of jealousy the tender shoots of merit will not grow.

The heart's wishes are like a horse galloping on the open sky. But alas, if one lacks the resources one cannot even bite the palm of one's own hand.
The old man's habit, his old woman knows.
When the coquette flirts with charm even the clay idol breaks out in smiles.
With familiarity even a tiger engenders no fear in a girl's heart.

TSONGA (Mozambique, South Africa)

Love is the one who enters someone's heart, even if it is taboo.

TURKANA (Kenya)

A poor man should only marry one wife, because many wives will cause him trouble.
An unmarried person in Turkanaland is called a fool.
Dancing is the way to make you famous and to get the girl you desire.
Money alone does not make a man rich.
The first wife always controls the co-wives in the household.

TURKEY

Before you love, learn to run through snow without leaving footprints.
For those in love, Baghdad is near Istanbul.

TWI (Ghana)

A good wife is more precious than gold.
A new marriage picks out the good yam.
A wife is not meant to be sent to someone else as a gift.
If jealousy caused hunger, then all men would be hungry.
If you have five wives, you have five different tongues.
It's love that makes the seashell stick to the rock.
Love is not based on wealth.
Love is the greatest of all virtues.
Nobody knows the secrets that exist between a husband and a wife.
The beauty of a woman is attributed to her husband.
Too many wives cause poverty, but it doesn't matter.

UKRAINE

A jealous woman keeps the whole house on fire.
A kiss tells more than a whole book.
A man has eyes to look; a woman has eyes to be looked at.
A man is the head of the household, but his wife is its soul.
An old woman without her mate is like borshch without bread.
By the time the wedding occurs your broken heart will be healed.
Give love free reign and it will lead you into slavery.
Gold and women rule the world.
He came to ask for her hand and returned with a pumpkin.
He who loves with his heart finds the words to say it.
Husband and wife, shout and fight, but the pillow brings them to-
gether.
If a man could survive without a woman, God would not have cre-
ated Eve.
If the eyes do not see, the heart does not cry.
If the heart is not in it the words will fool no one.
If you love me do not forget me; if you do not, do not mention me.
Let us eat borsch; as for the meat we will give each other a kiss.

Give love free reign and it will lead you into slavery. (Ukraine)

Love can neither be bought nor sold.
Love is impatient.
Love is like a good horse, it carries the man.
Love is worse than a sickness when it gives no peace.
Love understands all languages.
Lovers always find a place to meet.
May the borshch be meatless as long as I share it with my sweet
mate.
Sorrow is weightless; you carry your first love to your grave.
The eye runs to what is dear to the heart.
The road to a heart is only known by another heart.
Wealth begins with a wife.
Who loves well is ready to forgive.
You cannot hide light nor love.

UNITED STATES

A broken heart is like broken china: we can mend it, but we can
never erase the scars.
A heart without love is a violin without strings.
A loving heart is better and stronger than wisdom.
A man's heart at thirty is either steeled or broken.
A shotgun marriage won't last longer than the honeymoon.
A small love forgives much, a great love forgives little, and a perfect
love forgives all.
Choose your love, then love your choice.
He that gives the laws of love is usually a bachelor.
He who forces love where none is found remains a fool the whole
year round.
Hearts don't break, they bend and wither.
It is better to love someone you cannot have than have someone you
cannot love.
Let your heart rule your head in matters of affection.
Love and eggs should be fresh to be enjoyed.
Love and hate are the two closest emotions.

Love and the weather can never be depended upon. (United States)

Love and scandal are the best sweeteners of tea.
Love and the weather can never be depended upon.
Love can make any place agreeable.
Love cannot dwell with suspicion.
Love cures coquetry.
Love enters man through his eyes, woman through her ears.
Love intoxicates a man; marriage sobers him
Love is a friendship set afire.
Love is a little sighing and a little lying.
Many a heart is caught on the rebound.
Marriage and hanging go by destiny.
Marriage is a quick solution to more problems.
Marriage is like a tub of water: after a while, it is not so hot.
Nobody dies of a broken heart.
Once a lover, always a lover.
Tell me whom you love, and I'll tell you who you are.
The heart has arguments with which the understanding is unac-
quainted.
The heart has eyes that the brain knows nothing of.
The heart has no wrinkles.
The heart knows its own bitterness.
The sight of lovers feeds those in love.
The way to a man's heart is through his ego.
Those whom we love first we seldom wed.
True lovers are shy when people are by.
Two hearts never beat the same.
When love is greatest, words are fewest.

VIETNAM

When husband and wife live in harmony, they can dry up the ocean
without a bucket.
Jealousy does not grow old.
Let the heart that will not glow, slumber.
Perfect love sometimes does not come until the first grandchild.

WOLOF (Senegal, Gambia)

A lone hand does not applaud.
The look of love slices through all faults.

YAKA (Zaire)

A cock chases the rain with its tail, a woman shows her love towards
her husband in small-talk.
The heart is mad: it falls in love with one who is another's.
What a woman eats, a man eats too; what a man eats, so will a
woman.

YIDDISH

A good daughter is also a good daughter-in-law.
A mother understands what a child does not say.
All brides are beautiful. All dead are pious.
Between husband and wife only God is a judge.
By day they are ready to divorce, by night they are ready for bed.
For a little love you pay all your life.
From bad matches good children are also born.
Getting married takes an hour, but for a whole lifetime one has trou-
bles.
Husband and wife are like one flesh.
Husband and wife are one flesh but they possess two separate pock-
ets.
If one loves one's wife, then one loves her family too.
If the bride can't dance, she claims the musicians can't play.
If you are bitter at heart, sugar in the mouth will not help you.
If you're faithful to your wife, you'll have a healthy body.

When the wife is a queen, the husband is a king. (Yiddish)

It doesn't cost anything to promise and to love.
It is better to be embarrassed than heartbroken.
It's better to break off an engagement than to cancel a marriage contract.
It's never too late to die or get married.
Love and hunger don't dwell together.
Love is like butter, it's good with bread.
Love is sweet, but it's nice to have bread with it.
Love me less, but love me for a long time.
The heart is small and embraces the whole wide world.
The heart of a man may be compared to a sausage: no one can tell exactly what's inside.
Trouble cuts up the heart.
When an old man takes a young wife, he become young and she old.
When the bride is expecting, the wedding guests look away.
When the heart is full, the eyes overflow.
When the husband is a coachman, he is not afraid of his wife's curses.
When the wife is a queen, the husband is a king.
When you have a pretty wife, you are a bad friend.
When your destined spouse appears, you'll know it when you hear the first few spoken words.
Where there is love it never feels crowded.

YORUBA (Nigeria)

A husband is never too shy that he can't speak to his wife.
A king will not divorce a woman only for a poverty-stricken man to marry her.
A woman who has not lived with two husbands will never now which is the better.
Eyes never see a beautiful woman without greeting her.
He to whom a bride is being sought does not stretch his neck.
He who marries beauty marries trouble.

If you give a girl away in marriage with one hand, ten hands will not bring her back.
One does not strip a maiden of her clothes and sit gazing into her eyes.
One is never so desperate as to make one's sister one's wife.
The one you love is never blemished by disease.
What you handle gently is never spoiled; what you handle roughly causes grief.
White ants do not really love the dry stalk of corn: those we think love us, love us only a little.
You don't divorce someone who rides horses and then marry someone who walks on foot.

ZULU (South Africa)

A young man popular with the girls does not marry; old men do.
Love does not choose the blade of grass on which it falls.
Marriage is not divined for.

There is nothing in the world as sweet as love.
(Italy)

Bibliography

Andreyeva, Victoria. *Treasury of Russian Love Poems, Quotations & Proverbs in Russian and English*. New York: Hippocrene Books, 1995.

Awde, Nicholas. *Treasury of African Love Poems & Proverbs in the Languages of Africa and English*. New York: Hippocrene Books, 1997.

Bohm, Henry G. *A Handbook of Proverbs*. London: George Bell and Sons, 1904.

Branyon, Richard A. *Treasury of Roman Love Poems, Quotations & Proverbs in Latin and English*. New York: Hippocrene Books, 1995.

Carr, M.W. *A Collection of Telugu Proverbs*. New Delhi: Asian Educational Services, 1988.

Champion, Selwyn Gurney. *Racial Proverbs: A Selection of the World's Proverbs Arranged Linguistically*. London: Routledge & Kegan Paul, 1966.

Chavan, V.P. *The Konkani Proverbs*. New Delhi: Asian Educational Services, 1995.

de Ley, Gerd. *International Dictionary of Proverbs*. New York: Hippocrene Books, 1998.

Eisen, Armand. *The Heart's Song: Reflections on Love*. Kansas City, Missouri: Andrews and McNeel, 1995.

Gatto, Katherine Gyékényesi. *Treasury of Hungarian Love Poems, Quotations & Proverbs in Hungarian and English*. New York: Hippocrene Books, 1996.

Gross, David. *Treasury of Jewish Love Poems, Quotations & Proverbs in Yiddish, Hebrew, Ladino and English*. New York: Hippocrene Books, 1995.

———. *Dictionary of 1000 Jewish Proverbs*. New York: Hippocrene Books, 1997.

Hamilton, A.W. *Malay Proverbs*. Singapore: Times Editions Ltd., 1996.

Hille, Almut. *Treasury of German Love Poems, Quotations & Proverbs in German and English*. New York: Hippocrene Books, 1995.

Jensen, Herman. *A Classified Collection of Tamil Proverbs*. New Delhi: Asian Educational Services, 1993.

Kogos, Fred. *1001 Yiddish Proverbs*. New York: Carol Publishing Group, 1995.

Koul, Omkar N. *A Dictionary of Kashmiri Proverbs*. Patiala, India: Indian Institute of Language Studies, 1992.

Manwaring, A. *Marathi Proverbs*. New Delhi: Asian Educational Services, 1991.

Mertvago, Peter. *The Comparative Russian-English Dictionary of Russian Proverbs & Sayings*. New York: Hippocrene Books, 1995.

———. *Dictionary of 1000 French Proverbs with English Equivalents.* New York: Hippocrene Books, 1996.

———. *Dictionary of 1000 German Proverbs with English Equivalents.* New York: Hippocrene Books, 1997.

———. *Dictionary of 1000 Italian Proverbs with English Equivalents.* New York: Hippocrene Books, 1997.

Mieder, Wolfgang. *The Prentice-Hall Encyclopedia of World Proverbs.* Englewood Cliffs, New Jersey: Prentice-Hall, 1986.

Mieder, Wolfgang, Stewart A. Kingsbury, and Kelsie B. Harder. *A Dictionary of American Proverbs.* New York, Oxford: Oxford University Press, 1992.

Pemba, Lhamo. *Tibetan Proverbs.* Dharamsala, India: Library of Tibetan Works & Archives, 1996.

Rao, Narasinga. *A Handbook of Kannada Proverbs.* New Delhi: Asian Educational Services , 1994.

Serrano, Juan and Susan Serrano. *Treasury of Spanish Love Poems, Quotations & Proverbs in Spanish and English.* New York: Hippocrene Books, 1995.

Turkewicz-Sanko, Hélène. *Treasury of Ukrainian Love Poems, Quotations & Proverbs in Ukrainian and English.* New York: Hippocrene Books, 1997.

Vähämäki, Börje. *A Treasury of Finnish Love Poems, Quotations & Proverbs in Finnish, Swedish and English.* New York: Hippocrene Books, 1996.

Williams, Fionnuala. *Irish Proverbs.* Dublin: Poolbeg Press, 1992.

Also from Hippocrene Books . . .

Treasury of Love Quotations from Many Lands
compiled by the editors at Hippocrene
illustrated by Lizbeth Nauta

"Friendship after love is like smoke after a fire."
—*Magdalena Samozwaniec (Polish: 1899-1972)*

"Love is a reservoir of kindness and pleasure, like silos and pools during a seige."
—*Yehuda Amichai (Israeli: b. 1924)*

"O Love, love, love! Love is like a dizziness; It winna let a poor body gang about his biziness!"
—*James Hogg (Scottish: 1770-1835)*

Here is a one-of-a-kind collection of quotations on that ever inspiring subject— LOVE, from the hopeful and sentimental to the lovelorn and cynical. This charming gift volume contains over 500 quotations from 400 great writers, thinkers and personalities. These are words of wit and wisdom from all over the world (over 50 countries and regions), from antiquity to present day. With over 30 lovely illustrations throughout, this volume is the perfect gift of love for anyone.

140 pages • 6 x 9 • $17.50hc
0-7818-0574-0 • (673)

Bilingual Proverbs from Hippocrene . . .

These anthologies capture the rich language and culture of a region through the common proverbs of the day. The authors are accomplished writers, academics, and translators who share a common love of language.

The collections are organized:
- Alphabetically by key word
- With their English equivalents
- By English subject in an index

Dictionary of 1000 French Proverbs
Peter Mertvago
144 pages • 5 ½ x 8 ½
0-7818-0400-0 • $11.95pb • (146)

Dictionary of 1000 German Proverbs
Peter Mertvago
142 pages • 5 ½ x 8 ½
0-7818-0471-X • $11.95pb • (540)

Dictionary of 1000 Italian Proverbs
Peter Mertvago
144 pages • 5 ½ x 8 ½
0-7818-0458-2 • $11.95pb • (370)

Dictionary of 1000 Jewish Proverbs
David C. Gross
125 pages • 5 ½ x 8 ½
0-7818-0529-5 • $11.95pb • (628)

Dictionary of 1000 Polish Proverbs
Miroslaw Lipinski
144 pages • 5 ½ x 8 ½
0-7818-0482-5 • $11.95pb • (568)

Dictionary of 1,000 Russian Proverbs
Peter Mertvago
130 pages • 5 ½ x 8 ½
0-7818-0564-3 • $11.95pb • (694)

Dictionary of 1000 Spanish Proverbs
Peter Mertvago
160 pages • 5 ½ x 8 ½
0-7818-0412-4 • $11.95pb • (254)

*Also of Interest
from Hippocrene . . .*

A Classified Collection of Tamil Proverbs (Bilingual)
Rev. Herman Jensen
499 pages • 3,644 entries
0-7818-0592-9 • $19.95pb • (699)

International Dictionary of Proverbs
Gerd de Ley
Hardcover: 580 pages • 5 ½ x 8 ¼ • $29.50
Paperback: 580 pages • 5 ½ x 8 ¼ • $19.95

Dictionary of Proverbs and Their Origins
Roger and Linda Flavel
250 pages • 5 x 8
0-7818-0591-0 • $14.95pb • (701)

Bilingual Love Stories from Hippocrene . . .

Treasury of Classic French Love Short Stories
in French and English
edited by Lisa Neal
This beautiful gift volume includes six classic French love stories from Marie de France, Marguerite de Navarre, Madame de Lafayette, and Guy de Maupassant and others.
159 pages • 5 x 7
0-7818-0511-2 • $11.95hc • (621)

Treasury of Classic Spanish Love Short Stories
in Spanish and English
edited by Bonnie May
A lovely gift volume including five classic tales of love from Cervantes, Miguel de Unamuno, Jorge de Montemayor and Gustavo Adolfo Becquer among others.
157 pages • 5 x 7
0-7818-0512-0 • $11.95hc • (604)

Treasury of Classic Polish Love Short Stories
in Polish and English
edited by Miroslaw Lipinski
This volume delves into Poland's rich literary tradition to bring you classic love stories from five renowned authors. It explores love's many romantic, joyous, as well as melancholic facets.
109 pages • 5 x 7
0-7818-0513-9 • $11.95hc • (603)

Treasury of Classic Russian Love Short Stories
in Russian and English
by Anton Chekov
This beautiful new addition to the love stories series inlcudes three classic tales of love: "The Kiss," "Lady with a Lapdog," and "On Love," from Anton Chekov, noted nineteenth century Russian playwright and short story writer. The original Russian text is displayed side by side with its English translation.
128 pages • 5 x 7
0-7818-0601-1 • $11.95hc • (674)

Also available from Hippocrene . . .

Classic English Love Poems
edited by Emile Capouya
A charmingly illustrated gift edition which includes 95 classic poems of love from English writers.
130 pages • 6 x 9 • $17.50hc
0-7818-0572-4 • (671)

Classic French Love Poems
This volume contains over 25 beautiful illustrations by famous artist Maurice Leloir and 120 inspiring poems translated into English from French, the language of love itself.
130 pages • 6 x 9 • $17.50hc
0-7818-0573-2 • (672)

Hebrew Love Poems
edited by David C. Gross
Includes 90 love lyrics from biblical times to modern day, with illustrations by Shagra Weil.
91 pages • 6 x 9 • $14.95pb
0-7818-0430-2 • (473)

Irish Love Poems: Dánta Grá
edited by Paula Redes
This striking collection includes illustrations by Peadar McDaid and poems that span four centuries up to the most modern of poets, Nuala Ni Dhomhnaill, Brendan Kennelly, and Nobel prize winner, Seamus Heaney.
146 pages • 6 x 9 • $17.50hc
0-7818-0396-9 • (70)

Scottish Love Poems: A Personal Anthology
edited by Lady Antonia Fraser
Lady Fraser collects the loves and passions of her fellow Scots, from Burns to Aileen Campbell Nye, into a book that will find a way to touch everyone's heart.
253 pages • 5 ½ x 8 ¼ • $14.95pb
0-7818-0406-X • (482)

BILINGUAL LOVE POETRY

The newest additions to Hippocrene's bilingual series are filled with romantic imagery and philosophical musings. These beautiful gift volumes provide a glimpse into each culture's unique approach to affairs of the heart,
covering such subjects as eternal love, unrequited love and the pain of parting. Readings of most selections, performed by native speakers, are available on cassette audiobook (approximate running time: 2 hours).
All Books 128 pages • 5 x 7 • $11.95hc

TREASURY OF AFRICAN LOVE POEMS AND PROVERBS
Nicholas Awde, editor and translator
Selection of songs and sayings from numerous African languages, including Swahili, Yoruba, Berber, Zulu and Amharic.
0-7818-0483-3 • (611)

TREASURY OF ARABIC LOVE POEMS, QUOTATIONS AND PROVERBS
Farid Bitar, editor and translator
Selections from Adonis, Kahlil Gibran, Saïd `Aql, and Fadwä Tüqän.
0-7818-0395-0 • (71)

TREASURY OF CZECH LOVE POEMS, QUOTATIONS AND PROVERBS
Marcela Rýdlová-Ehrlich, editor and translator
Among the 40 poets represented are Bohumil Hrabal, Milan Kundera, Jan Neruda and Nobel prize winner Jaroslav Seifert.
0-7818-0571-6 • (670)

TREASURY OF FINNISH LOVE POEMS, QUOTATIONS AND PROVERBS
Börje Vähämäki, editor and translator
Selections from Alekis Kivi, Eeva Kilpi, Johann Runeberg and Edith Södergran.
0-7818-0397-7 • (118)

TREASURY OF FRENCH LOVE POEMS, QUOTATIONS AND PROVERBS
Richard A. Branyon, editor and translator
Selections from Baudelaire, Hugo, Rimbaud and others.
0-7818-0307-1 • (344)
Audiobook: 0-7818-0359-4 • $12.95 • (580)

TREASURY OF GERMAN LOVE POEMS, QUOTATIONS AND PROVERBS
Alumut Hille, editor
Selections from Schiller, Goethe, Rilke and others.
0-7818-0296-2 • (180)
Audiobook: 0-7818-0360-8 • $12.95 • (577)

TREASURY OF HUNGARIAN LOVE POEMS, QUOTATIONS AND PROVERBS
Katherine Gyékenyesi Gatto, editor and translator
0-7818-0477-9 • (550)

TREASURY OF ITALIAN LOVE POEMS, QUOTATIONS AND PROVERBS
Richard A. Branyon, editor and translator
Selections by Dante Aligheri, Petrarch and Pugliese are included.
0-7818-0352-7 • (587)
Audiobook: 0-7818-0366-7 • $12.95 • (581)

TREASURY OF JEWISH LOVE POEMS, QUOTATIONS AND PROVERBS, in Hebrew, Yiddish and Ladino
David Gross, editor
Includes selections from Bialik and Halevi.
0-7818-0308-X • (346)
Audiobook: 0-7818-0363-2 • $12.95 • (579)

TREASURY OF POLISH LOVE POEMS, QUOTATIONS AND PROVERBS

Miroslaw Lipinski, editor and translator
Works by Krasinski, Sienkiewicz and Mickiewicz are included among 100 selections by 44 authors.
0-7818-0297-0 • (185)
Audiobook: 0-7818-0361-6 • $12.95 • (576)

TREASURY OF ROMAN LOVE POEMS, QUOTATIONS AND PROVERBS

Richard A. Branyon, editor and translator
Includes works by Cicero, Ovid and Horace.
0-7818-0309-8 • (348)

TREASURY OF RUSSIAN LOVE POEMS, QUOTATIONS AND PROVERBS

Victorya Andreyeva, editor
Includes works by Tolstoy, Chekhov and Pushkin.
0-7818-0298-9 • (591)
Audiobook: 0-7818-0364-0 • $12.95 • (586)

TREASURY OF SPANISH LOVE POEMS, QUOTATIONS AND PROVERBS

Juan and Susan Serrano, editors
Includes works by de la Vega, Calderon and Garcia Marquez.
0-7818-0358-6 • (589)
Audiobook: 0-7818-0365-9 • $12.95 • (584)

TREASURY OF UKRAINIAN LOVE POEMS, QUOTATIONS AND PROVERBS

edited by Hélène Turkewicz-Sanko
Among the poets included are Marusia Churai, Ivan Kotliarevsky, Taras Stevchenko, Ivan Franko and Lesia Ukrainka.
0-7818-0517-1 • (650)

All prices subject to change. **TO PURCHASE HIPPOCRENE BOOKS** contact your local bookstore, call (718) 454-2366, or write to: HIPPOCRENE BOOKS, 171 Madison Avenue, New York, NY 10016. Please enclose check or money order, adding $5.00 shipping (UPS) for the first book and $.50 for each additional book.